Deer Bleating Sound Yo Yo

——The Story of the Countryside People

——Behold A Rainbow

◎ Lin Yeh Lien

天空數位圖書出版

Author's Preface

This book belongs to biographical literature and is named "*Deer Bleating Sound Yo Yo*" because it is related to the place name of my hometown; It is also related to the sentences in *The Book of Songs*, which is the academic field I specialize in. This book is divided into two parts. The first part, "*The Story of the Countryside People*", is a brief record of the place where I grew up and the process of my growth; because my childhood was in Nantou, this place made me realize extremely unforgettable experiences, and enjoy maximum happiness. The second part: "*Behold a Rainbow*" is a self narration of my emotional expe-riences during my master's program. Most of the length was completed in 1984, with a small portion being recently supple-mented; The reason why this manuscript has been put on hold until now is because people are constantly learning and growing, and the adjustment of their thoughts and emotions is also the same; Like bananas and papayas, they must wait until they are ripe before they can be eaten.

Regarding the content mentioned in the book, I adhere to the principle of "not writing unless it is true", so there are almost no exaggerated or creative expressions, and in fact, there is no mood to add any creativity. The second unit particularly touched me deeply, as I always felt that the matter of making a girlfriend has caused great trauma to the honor, body, and soul of myself and my family, which is unexpected. Fortunately, the rain passed and the sky cleared, and I passed the test safely. I will retire at the age of 65 next year. With this book, I can at least witness that I was once young, not only through certain experiences, but also leaving traces.

I remember Qijun once described in his article "*About Oranges Becoming Red*": "If I don't write anymore, won't my beloved loved ones and elders' unforgettable pain, silently resigned suffering and sacrifice be forever

unknown to the world? How can I be reconciled? How can I not feel indebted to them?" Ordinary people also have the reason to "cherish their own worn-out brooms", so they may write down their life experiences around them and keep some personal life records. I recall my life journey since childhood. Nantou, Changhua, Yunlin, Da'an District of Taipei, and Taoyuan Guishan District are all closely related to my residential life, each with many of my footprints and leaving profound memories. And this book is particularly based on the details of Nantou's hometown, and then adds other growth experiences, because on the eve of retirement, it wants to express the intention of returning to roots after falling leaves. There are beautiful parts that can make me relive; The unpleasant parts are available for me to review and improve. Anyway, experiencing one thing can increase some wisdom, and I hope that in the future, everything will develop towards a beautiful and good outcome.

A peaceful life is an unparalleled happiness, and my thoughts have always been like this. I almost never compete with others for anything; After retirement, life can definitely be more peaceful. In my mind, only reading and Tai Chi Chuan are the two activities that can make me feel the happiest. The joy and satisfaction in my heart are like drinking water, and only the person who drinks water knows the temperature best. Therefore, I am mentally prepared to become a happy elderly person.

Lin Yeh Lien respectfully wrote at
the Institute of Sinology at
National Yunlin University of Science & Technology
October 2023

Table of Contents

1. The Hometown of Deer

(1) A place for salt merchants to breathe a sigh of relief

Luming, formerly known as Lukuit, was located in Buxia Village, Mingjian Township, Nantou County. Buxia Village is composed of two major villages, the eastern half is Buxia with lower terrain; the western half is Luming with a relatively high terrain.

Since ancient times, "people will not go hundreds of miles to sell firewood, nor will they go thousands of miles to sell rice", because people do not engage in unprofitable transactions. However, salt is an irreplaceable daily necessity, so salt merchants must set off from Lugang in Changhua and work hard to carry salt to sell in the Nantou area, even deep into mountainous, like Puli. On the way, there is a resting place for merchants, where many people are used to replacing worn-out straw sandals. Over time, a small hill of straw sandals is formed, which is why this place is called "Grass Shoes Dun", which is today's Caotun.

Nantou County is famous for its many mountains, salt merchants from Lugang must travel long distances and cross mountains and ridges; Although facing the lush green mountains, most of them have no intention of watching. They only know that for the sake of life and sales, no matter how deep mountains and wild fields are worth moving forward. The business route always twists and turns along the foot of the mountain, which is generally not particularly difficult; However, shortly after departing from Changhua County, when they arrived at Qingshui Rock in Shetou Township, they had to face a severe test.

To be honest, how could those "people at the foot of the mountain" who want to make money from the "mountaintop people" escape the challenge of mountaineering? The test is to carry heavy loads and cross the mountain road.

The mountain road is called the "Eighteen Bends Ancient Road". It starts from Qingshui Rock and is a typical narrow road. The gravel road winds up without railings. Cars cannot pass, only for pedestrians to walk on, especially at the end of the ancient road, which is even steeper. They carried heavy burdens, overcame difficulties and obstacles, and arrived at the top panting. Facing the suddenly enlightened new scene, they not only felt relieved, but also felt like they had regained their vitality. Here they entered Nantou County, and immediately a small Tudigong Temple came into sight. However, during the Qing Dynasty, here was still a dense and lush forest. Slowly descending eastward, this village was called Lukuit. If it's a clear day with thousands of miles of sky, here they could point to the magnificent Central Mountains, as well as Yushan and Alishan located on the southeast side.

(2) Renamed from Lukuit to Luming

From the undeveloped period until the Qing Dynasty, the Lukuit area was always a place with dense forests. The most common animals wandering or jumping among the woods are wild deer, mountain Qiang, monkeys, bamboo pheasants, pangolins, civets, and hares. This place originally had two adjacent ponds, which later merged into one and became known as Hulu Pond or Hulu Cave; The pronunciation of 'Hulu' is exactly the meaning of 'gourd' in Chinese. The term "Kuit" in Minnan language originally meant a cave or depression, while the "water Kuit" in Minnan dialect means a "pond". This gourd shaped pond is a place where wild deer and other animals drink water on weekdays, so this place and this pond are both referred to as "Lukuit". The pronunciation of "Lu" precisely means "deer" in Chinese. If we only talk about "deer", the name "Lukuit" means: deer cave, or deer's nest, is also a deer's drinking pool.

The north of Lukuit is a row of barrier hills -- Hengshan. The village in the south was famous for producing deer skin, so it is called Pizai Liao and later renamed Jinzi Village. Walking southeast from Lukuit for about thirty

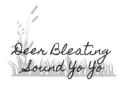

Parents are forced to accept the wave after wave of the Japanese government's vigorous promotion of the imperial nationalization movement, while considering the immediate practical benefits, hoping that the next generation can quickly learn useful knowledge in order to become competitive in society when they grow up.

Over the years, almost all newborns here have taken Japanese names, children are studying Japanese at school, and adults have to use Japanese to move around in society. They have almost reached the point where they cannot buy tickets without speaking Japanese, and they are unable to negotiate official business. Everyone understands the social reality of "Japanese language is versatile" and "Chinese language is useless". When learning Japanese is urgently needed, who would waste time getting in touch with traditional Chinese culture? Since one does not know Chinese culture, it is impossible to have a deep understanding of inherent traditional virtues. They only know to listen to the words of "Sir" (police officer) and to be loyal to the Japanese Emperor.

It's a pity that the family who taught Chinese language with sincerity and dedication, due to the advanced age of the teacher in this generation, did not have as much physical strength as before. According to common sense, he should often sit at the top and be well received. However, in the busy and competitive reality of society, those who are outdated and useless are often neglected, which makes him constantly lament: "What is the use of studying a lifetime's classics?" As an old and frail man, he is only occasionally invited to the halls of certain households, holding a small calligraphy brush, and slowly helping others copy the names on ancestral tablets; Eventually, he walked down the stage of life in a state of sadness and silence.

My father grew up with busy farming at home and didn't have the opportunity to go to school. He could only watch as his two brothers had the opportunity to learn Japanese and envied other boys of the same age in the village who could enter Japanese schools. Unfortunately, when my father was fourteen years old, my grandfather was washed away by the flood. After my father became an orphan, farming became busier and harder, but he knew how to go to the Chinese language teacher during his leisure time, borrow books from him, and request guidance, so he became a person who had never entered school but could read Chinese books.

When my father was a child, he worked in the fields and could fluently recite the titles of twenty chapters of *The Analects*: "*Xue Er*, First" "*Wei Zheng*, Second," "*Ba Yi*, Third," "*Li Ren*, Fourth," "*Gong Ye Chang*, Fifth"......"*Yao Yue*, Twentieth". But when my uncles heard what my father had memorized, they all laughed at him and thought what era it is now, how could he pack a lot of useless things in his stomach? It's a waste of time and it also shows that the reciter's mind is a bit dull. At the same time, mocking him for not understanding Japanese, he will lose a lot in the future.

The books my father read were borrowed from the Chinese language teacher, with many red cinnabar dots between the lines. In my father's view, he can identify Chinese word, is no longer an illiterate. Moreover, such as "*The Sage of the Past*" and "*A Must Read in Life*", as well as many Min Nan dialect song books, mostly promote the spirit of loyalty, filial piety, moral integrity, and righteousness. He firmly believed that it was very valuable spiritual food. The so-called 'model in the ancients' means that the moral cultivation of future generations can be self constructed by studying ancient books.

It was later confirmed that those in the village who despised traditional Chinese culture and were eager to climb to Japan could hardly find the temperament of gentleness. They were full of momentum, advanced and trendy, and they advocate utilitarianism. Unconsciously, the honest and beautiful customs of Lukuit had undergone a qualitative change. This was a

After walking around the village and completing the worship, some children always like to walk down the Eighteen Bend Ancient Salt Road. If they have heard adults tell about the history of this ancient road, then besides busy searching for clear springs and crabs halfway, they will also have a sincere admiration for their ancestors and elders.

(5) My Rural Childhood

The Taiwanese pronunciation of "獵鴞" is "la hyou", which means "an eagle that can hunt down other birds". There is a saying in Minnan dialect that goes, "Some people don't keep the hen tightly closed, but keep blaming the 獵鴞 for catching the chick." It is advised that people should know how to review their own mistakes and not just blame others. On weekdays in the village, you can often hear the urgent shouts of children in the distance in Minnan language: "ˌla 'e hyou - clamp, clamp, clamp." "ˌla 'e hyou - clamp, clamp, clamp." In an instant, all the children in the village mobilized and rushed out of the door one after another, shouting in unison: "ˌla 'e hyou - clamp, clamp, clamp." This momentum rose to the sky, shaking the wind and clouds until the hovering eagle disappeared without a trace, the danger of the chickens was relieved, and the children were willing to stop their troops and enter the house.

Bagua Terrace, also known as Bagua Mountains, starts from Changhua in the north, passes through Shetou Township, and ends at the north bank of Choushui River in Mingjian Township of Nantou County in the south. This mountain range is famous for its eagles, mainly the gray faced buzzard. From the area of Qingshui Rock in Shetou Township, flying into the village of Luming, chickens are the most likely victims. Write a poem titled "Hunting Eagle" here and record its situation:

> Leaving the ground and soaring into the sky,
> gracefully hovering,

the eagle's fiery eyes disdained a single blink.

Children quickly rushed out of the door,

from the village head to the village end,

the sound of "clip clip" was everywhere.

In the northeast corner of Hulu Pond, there is a Tudigong Temple. Since the Qing Dynasty, our Lin family has dedicated the land in front of the right side of the Tudigong Temple as a pool for the buffalo in the village to soak in the water for summer. Especially in midsummer, this pool is the favorite of the buffalo. Melia azedarach is planted on the shore. Every spring and summer, purple flowers bloom and emit a faint fragrance. There are several wooden stakes nailed to the ground to tie up the buffalos soaking in water. When it comes to the dry season in winter, water buffalo don't have to soak in water because it's cold. As soon as the day for catching fish arrives, adults and children come to the mud with buckets to catch Chinese yellow eels, loaches, soil lice…… and so on. The adults and children struggle to pull them out of the mud, screaming loudly, very exciting!

Starting from May each year, the Fraxinus griffithii tree attracts many unicorns (The rhinoceros beetle), dark red, brown, and black. The male beetle has long horns symbolizing majesty on its head; Females have no horns on their heads and their bodies are not shiny. They come here to suck on tree sap, which is a living textbook for ecological learning. As for the orange red back, black belly, shiny whole body, and long snouted Bamboo shoot weevil, which is notorious for biting bamboo shoots, children often grill them to eat. On fruit trees such as peaches and plums, as well as the acacia confusa tree (scientific name: Acacia confusa) full of golden flowers, there are countless beetles that inhabit crops. For crops, they are pests; If you shake the branches a few times, they will fall all over the ground; Some of them only pretend to be dead, have wings but do not fly, so children easily fill bamboo tubes and take them home. To protect the esophagus of ducks, each beetle must be knocked.

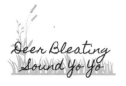

produced can be picked up and carried to the foot of the mountain for sale. It was once an important resource for the local people to rely on for a living. The most common weed under the tree is broad-leaved duck tongue (scientific name: Spermacoe latifolia Aublet), which is commonly referred to in Minnan dialect as the "Grass Pi Ah". Its leaves have fine fuzz, making it the best material for making a bed for water buffaloes. Between July and November each year, villagers often use their spare time from busy farming to go to the forests high in Hengshan to hoe the "Grass Pi Ah", which is a kind of grass that cattle and sheep do not eat. The left and right piles of grass are scattered everywhere, allowing them to dry on the mountain. Then, the villagers slightly modified the bullock cart and replaced the left rear large wheel with an iron sheet wheel. Before going down the mountain, they also need to tie the iron wheel with thick ropes to prevent it from rotating. Then, they can use the bullock cart to gradually transport hay down the mountain and return to their own courtyard, building a small hill as high as the roof. In the coming year, the buffalo's bedding grass will be enough without worrying. Because of this, after weeding, the bottom of the Hengshan forest is usually clean, rather than overgrown with weeds.

In the lazy afternoon, the earth was covered in golden yellow, and the little boys were all sunburned into little black boys. They often ran forward quickly and rushed directly to the hay mound in the courtyard, as if standing at the top of a cliff, breathing in the fragrance of hay, jumping excitedly, looking around, shouting loudly: "I stand the tallest in Taiwan." However, they were always ignored.

Below the mountainside, the green grass is thick and soft, like a mat, interspersed with many small flowers. There is a road wide enough for two ox carts to meet, leading directly from the village to the foot of the mountain; Several tall trees stand on the roadside, their branches swaying in the wind, as if fanning for the hardworking villagers. The herding families in the village drive their cattle and sheep to the grazing area halfway up Hengshan to eat grass every day. Children are likely to carry a mysterious item prepared in advance at home, which is made from the phloem of the root of the jade leaf golden flower (scientific name: Mussaenda pubescens), crushed and rinsed to form a small ball of cicada catching adhesive. It is held in the mouth and a small piece of bamboo stick is exposed outside; Holding a long bamboo pole and leaning against his shoulder, he smiled and drove the cattle and goat up the mountain.

Whenever the setting sun is about to disappear and the dusk is cool, a large number of cattle and goat return from the mountainside, occupying the entire road. The scene is very spectacular, like a victorious army returning. On the road and when meeting them, pedestrians will voluntarily yield to the roadside. Sometimes I see shepherds returning with high toes and silent mouths, but walking with a lively spirit, because they carry many spoils of war. In addition to the black cicadas, there may also be large beehives, bird nests, or rabbits, civets, or bamboo chickens caught in traps. Sometimes he would show off to people, saying that he and a few children caught snakes together and ate roasted snake meat; And bring back the complete snake skin with fine sand inside, which can also be considered one of the toys.

Sometimes, children come back from the mountain with a large cardboard box in their hands, containing some branches and leaves of the Jiang Mou Tree (scientific name: Schefflera octophylla). There are several large white insects on the leaves, and there are several long, soft, but not stinging large needles all over the body. He is preparing to welcome the emperor moth (scientific name: Attacus atlas) that emerges from its pupa in a few days. The wings of the emperor moth are mainly orange in color, paired with many changing patterns, making them very colorful.

There are also some children in the corner of the courtyard, inspecting the branches and leaves of Du Ying (scientific name: Elaeocarpus sylvestris), which

were transported back using a bullock cart a few days ago. There are many fruits between the branches and leaves, and after placing them in the courtyard for a few days, the Du Ying fruit naturally ripens; Some children are focused on finding fruits and eating with relish.

"Aside, aside, aside!" A little boy slightly lowered his pants, took out the treasure, and urinated while walking, shouting to pedestrians to make way immediately. Then stop and look back at the long urine trail left in the middle of the road, evaluating whether it looks like buffalo urine released while pulling the car.

The little girls were busy with their own tasks, with some holding the fruit of the Golden Dew Flower (scientific name: Duranta erecta) in their hands, which was clusters of orange beads, sparkling and dazzling. Someone picked several plants of Showa grass (scientific name: Crassocephalum crepidioides), whose flowers resembled small bells. Some girls are also busy searching for the black fruit of Qianfan Teng (scientific name: Polygonum chinense L.), and eating it, their lips are all dyed black.

At the moment when the sun was tilted, the woman and child took a basket of eggs from the brooding hen's nest and entered the house. They closed the two wooden doors, leaving a small transparent gap. The mother and son took turns bringing the eggs to the transparent line. This is to test the phased results of hens hatching eggs and see if there are "red veins" inside; If there is, feel happy; Repeatedly passing through the light line, if the "red veins" are not visible, one will say in frustration, "Wow! This has no shape". Those "without shape" can be cooked for pigs to eat before they turn into stinky eggs. Tangible, leave it to the hen to continue working hard. The mother will also remind the child, "The rooster from next door is here, don't drive it away, otherwise our eggs will have no embryonic form."

3. Greed, anger, and delusion within the clan

During the Japanese occupation period, my grandparents were a large family composed of three major families: elder granduncle, grandfather, and younger granduncle. My younger granduncle has been officially recognized by the Japanese authorities as a "Bao Zheng"; This identity, under this special high-pressure rule, appears to have a relatively strong momentum.

My grandfather often goes up the mountain to work. Once, he led a buffalo and encountered a big flood. He accidentally stepped into an already overflowing ditch at the foot of the mountain, and was washed away and died. Leave three sons and four daughters behind. My father was only fourteen years old at that time, and my youngest aunt was only eight years old. Both of my elder uncles received education from schools set up by the Japanese, while my father never went to school. According to my father said, because the farming was very busy at that time, my grandfather did not let him go to school and planned to distribute more land as compensation in the future. But since my grandfather passed away early, the promise of distributing more land fell through.

My grandfather has passed away, but the situation of the three households merging into one still persists. Among them, the family without parent will inevitably suffer losses, such as some people taking public funds to the foot of the mountain to secretly purchase paddy fields and create personal wealth for themselves, but conceal it.

My grandfather has left, and neither my father nor my youngest aunt has entered the school. They have been bullied the most, and their trait is loyalty and honesty. Er Bo[2] is naturally intelligent but very domineering, even his

---

[2] "Er Bo" is the literal translation of "my father's second elder brother" in Minnan dialect according to pronunciation.

widowed mother is afraid of him; He is essentially the head of this household, with several sisters almost praising him as the emperor, except for my youngest aunt, who silently supports each other with my father.

During World War II, my father quickly got married and was transferred to Nanyang by the Japanese authorities as a cooking soldier. During the four-year service period, the Japanese authorities sent welfare benefits to Lukuit, but when my father returned home from the military, he found that the so-called welfare had been completely used up and had not been received at all; Er Bo said that those were all benefits that grandmother should receive, but in reality, they were possessed by Er Bo. In addition, before returning home from the military, the Japanese government forced Taiwanese soldiers to deposit cash in Japanese banks, so my father only returned to Taiwan with a few deposit receipts. Later, Japan unconditionally surrendered to China. Can the deposit slips held by Taiwan veterans be cashed? Japan has been ignoring it for a long time.

Originally, the Lin family was considered a prosperous family in this village, not without money, but my father was very poor. After his discharge from the army, my father went to the Chenghuang Temple in Nantou to ask for the divine sign. The man who explained the divine sign seemed to be able to tell fortune, saying, "At the age of twenty-four, you divide your family property, and at the age of twenty-five, you are no different from a beggar." Later, my father often spoke highly of the divine sign of the City God at that time, which was very effective.

The distribution of property is based on the existing land in the Luming area, with the three major households of the grandparents equally distributed; As for the father's generation, each of the three brothers received one share, plus the grandmother's share, so it was divided into four shares; My grandmother once hugged my second elder sister, but she passed away soon after; In fact, the land belonging to my grandmother later became the private property of Er Bo. For a moment, it used to seem like a thriving big family in a place, but my father didn't have much land and had almost no cash.

I have a big brother who died young before the age of one. Later, I had four elder sisters and one younger sister, and all six of us had good relationships. When she was a child, my eldest sister met the poorest stage of my family. She often lacked food during meals. She could only pour a drop of peanut oil and add a drop of soy sauce, and that was all. Sometimes, she couldn't get even a drop of peanut oil. She was clamoring for a drop of peanut oil. My mother was troubled because there was not much oil left, so she wanted to keep it for cooking. My father said, "Just give her a gesture, just a gesture." My elder sister didn't know what that meant. Later, she once shouted several times, "I want a gesture, I want a gesture." The next door people could also hear this ridiculous noise.

My younger granduncle serves as the "Bao Zheng" under the jurisdiction of the Japanese government and has a good reputation in the local area. He has three sons, and the eldest son is very outstanding. As a matchmaker, my mother introduced a good woman from her hometown, Zhuwei Village, to my uncle as their daughter-in-law. But the traditional mother-in-law is very authoritarian, and the grandaunt doesn't cherish her daughter-in-law, which is probably similar to the story of "*Peacock Flies Southeast*". Once, when the New Year was approaching, my grandaunt angrily scolded her daughter-in-law and kicked her out of the house, causing her to run back to her parents' house. As a result, her eldest son committed suicide by hanging himself in the room where the ox cart was placed. Afterwards, my mother no longer dared to help people as matchmakers.

At that time, the restroom was located behind the house and was very old. If it rains, the children had to pass through Er Bo's house to avoid getting caught in the rain. Once, as my third elder sister was about to go home after using the restroom, Er Bo's family deliberately closed the door and refused to let her pass. My third elder sister stood outside his house crying and shouting until my father personally went to bring her back. Later, my father simply used a sledgehammer to make a big hole in the wall of the cowshed for his own children to enter and exit. From then on, there was no need to pass through Er Bo's house on rainy days. My father always said, "Fortunately, we have a very obedient female cow, and even the youngest child can walk over without any worries."

Er Bo gave birth to a total of three sons and five daughters, and My Second Elder Male Cousin's personality is very similar to Er Bo. One cousin is the same age as me, and two younger cousins are younger than me. Once, a few children were playing by the Hulu Pond. My older sister was crouching towards the pond, digging for clay. My Second Elder Male Cousin walked over and stepped on her back with one foot, saying, "Kick you down." My second sister was very angry and ran over to relieve the danger.

On the connected hillside, my family's land is above and Er Bo's land is below. He intentionally planted a row of bamboo on the adjacent boundary, and the bamboo roots continued to extend upwards, causing the boundary to migrate. Later on, my father managed to buy land elsewhere to escape their interference, because other landlords were not so easy to bully.

When the sky turns white like a fish belly, my mother goes to the mountain to dig tree heads. After breakfast, my father carries the tree heads and goes to Shetou Township at the foot of the mountain to sell. When he returned home before noon, he began to do his own farm work. The job of digging tree heads is often the job that my mother did during her pregnancy. Until one day, when my father finished selling tree heads in the Shetou Township, the buyer invited him to eat a bowl of glutinous rice balls. My father suddenly thought that the work of digging and selling tree heads should have come to a successful end! From then on, he never picked anything to go down the mountain and sell.

One day, our pregnant sow died, and a loess footprint could be seen vaguely on her belly. This is too scary; my parents think we should try to move out of this terrible place. After private discussions, my younger granduncle and my father decided to move out of this old house together and build a new house in another location.

The new house is built in the middle of the quiet countryside, which is 5 minutes' walk away from the old house. It is a standard Sanheyuan. In order to be cautious, we specially request the Guanyin Bodhisattva (Divine Spirit) of Jintian Temple to indicate the central point, which is generally agreed upon by both uncle and nephew. This central point is the hall where the gods and ancestral tablets are worshipped together. A virtual dividing line can be drawn to distinguish the left and right sides of the Sanheyuan. Younger granduncle is considered an elder, choosing the position of respect and living by the Dragon's Side; My father is a younger generation and lives by the Tiger's Side. In 1962, we moved into the new home. From then on, we can stay away from Er Bo and his family, and finally let go of the big stone in our hearts.

The door couplets in the hall of the new house are carved and write, "Migrating from Zhangpu to the overseas 'Yingzhou' (It is a legendary overseas fairy mountain, referring to Taiwan), following the teachings of our ancestors, inheriting the teachings of Confucius and Mencius, to establish the

foundation of the country. "Fortunately, when I was in junior high school, I knew the meaning of it; Knowing the meaning will produce a motivational effect.

The little aunt who married to Tianzi Village often comes back to her parents' house during holidays and festivals. She really likes our new home. Once, after walking for 40 minutes with three gifts, she returned to our new home and sat down to eat during lunch time. Unexpectedly, in a moment, Er Bo angrily walked in, grabbed her bowls and ordered her to come to his house first. She went to his house with tears in her eyes, holding the other two gifts. Er Bo seemed to think that when the married sister returned to her mother's house, if she didn't make his home the first stop and report to him first, which was simply disrespectful to him.

In 1962, my younger granduncle and my father moved into the new home. My younger granduncle brought his two sons and many grandchildren into the new home. Younger granduncle's family owns half, and we live in the other half. We could live in peace, but the relationship between the two sides seems to be not as good as expected. The children in our family have received many awards from elementary school and pasted them on the walls of our small living room. Their children do not have any awards, which may make them feel jealous.

When I was in junior high school, there once a time when we were watching TV and someone hanged himself. My fourth sister said, "He hanged himself." My father heard this nearby and suddenly ran over and shouted, "Shut up." My fourth sister felt confused and didn't know the reason for being blamed. Later on, we learned that there was a tragic incident where our uncle committed suicide by hanging himself before we could see it. We also heard our mother talk to father: "It seems that their resentment has not dissipated yet." Since the tragedy of their eldest son hanging himself in the old house in the past, my grandaunt has only kept a low profile, swallowed her anger, and even feared her two daughters in law, making it even more difficult for her heart to dissipate a sense of sorrow.

Later, two uncles who lived across the yard repeatedly complained to my father, "You have taken all of the Feng Shui of this house." My father only replied coldly, "What kind of Feng Shui is that? I can't even take a break at noon while working." My father usually gives in to the behavior of his uncle and his family everywhere. For example, they privately force workers to make the gate composed of two red brick exterior walls one high and one low. The brick wall on our side of the gate is significantly lower than theirs. My father never criticized anything, and we never wanted to take advantage of them for our own benefit. Whenever I pick up a big broom to clean the courtyard, I not only clean our half that separated by the virtual center line in front of the hall, but also sweep up the garbage on their half.

Around 1970, my younger granduncle passed away. One day in 2007, two people living across from each other, Second younger Uncle and his nephew, representing the two households, suddenly walked into my living room for some reason. They held the document in their hands and handed it directly to me, saying, "This is the map file I applied which is our residential land." I took a brief look and was quite shocked because it recorded that my family's ownership was one-third. I immediately said, "This is not right. Our family should own half of it, and the other half should be shared equally between you two households." They didn't say a word, took back the documents, and turned around and left. I remember when I was three years old, this land was jointly built by my father and his uncle. At that time, it was

agreed that each household would hold half of it. After my younger granduncle passed away, someone secretly changed my ownership to one-third. But the fact that there has never been a sale or gift between each other, how could the land ownership and distribution ratio be quietly changed, while our family is completely unaware.

Later, I said to my three sons: "At present, the area of the property on our ownership certificate is calculated based on one-third, which is incorrect. We should have owned half of it. However, my uncle lives opposite, and I don't want to sue them. The virtual line drawn on the center line of the hall is the boundary between us and them. It has always been like this. If our holding is not half, how could we have lived like this for decades without any objections from them, but now they are using dark tactics in writing, which may add some trouble to the future."

Not long after, second younger Uncle accidentally fell down the tree while picking lychees, and injured his back neck. Afterwards, they invited a foreign caregiver to take care of him. The issue of property ownership can only be put on hold and we look forward to a successful resolution in the future.

4. Happy New Residence

My parents' eldest son passed away before he was one year old. They later gave birth to four daughters in a row, only to have another boy, who was me. I was born less than 10 days ago, and I was already 2 years old. Traditional algorithms are really unique. My family cherishes me very much. When choosing a name for me, my mother was dissatisfied with any name my father chose for me; My father had no choice but to go to Jintian Temple and ask a divine shaman to name me for me, and my mother had nothing to say. But when my father took the name given by the divine shaman and went to the township office to register, the staff had a disagreement. After their discussion, they suggested a slight change, so they registered my current name for me. Therefore, if someone asks me, "How did you get your name?" I think the standard answer should be: "The staff of the township office and my father discussed it based on the opinions of the divine shaman." My eldest sister was ten years older than me. At that time, my mother was very proud, because when I was born, all the sesame oil chicken my mother ate during confinement was cooked by my eldest sister.

My father no longer picked things and went down the mountain to sell. In order to start farming, he had to borrow sugarcane receipts from several relatively affluent households in the village, similar to loans, to prepare for these farming funds in order to purchase seedlings, fertilizers, and so on, and start farming. After the harvest of crops, he withdrew the cash and returned to the village. He must repay each household first before entering the house. That is his principle of being a good person.

When I moved to the new house, I was three years old. A few neighbor children and our own siblings were carrying chairs and other items together, passing through a small forest and walking on a slightly curved slope. My cousin, who had a shiny bald head, was pecked twice by a swooping bird from the branch. Everyone screamed and escorted him safely to our new house.

My father was focused on farming in his own field. I remember when I was in high school, he had already purchased nearly seven hectares of land. We usually don't hire workers because the whole family is very hardworking, and besides, my father's physical strength is particularly good, and he doesn't even need to rest at noon. Of course, our family property cannot be compared to that of the elder granduncle's sons. They have a lot of land, and someone of

them raise 6 water buffaloes at home, sometimes hiring nearly 10 laborers to farm together.

Our whole family is very hardworking, starting from early morning every day. The older sisters take turns getting up every morning to cook breakfast for the whole family. As for the younger sisters and brother, we allocated a fixed number of rooms as cleaning areas, with a total of seven commonly used rooms to be cleaned. My mother wiped the tables and chairs with a duster, and fed the cattle, pigs, chickens, ducks, cats and dogs with my father. The children finished our respective tasks, had breakfast, and then carried backpacks to school. When we return home in the evening, my sisters will only work more than they did in the morning. Everyone enjoys it and never complains about hard work.

During dinner, it was very peaceful, and those who had eaten their fill left the table first. Sometimes, my mother, me, and two sisters were left eating. After a while, there was a sudden clattering sound. Both sisters quickly scooped their food into their mouths, and I stared straight at them. Then they almost simultaneously put down their bowls and chopsticks and said, "Wash the dishes," with their mouths bulging and pointing at each other. My mother always smiles and eats more slowly with me.

If I have free time at home, I always lead our buffalo to graze on the field path. Our buffalo should not meet another's cattle because some buffaloes are prone to fight. They would hit each other with their horns as they ran, which is often not a problem that children can solve. So, whenever two buffalo owners see each other from afar, the best way is to pull one of the buffalos to a sugarcane field, cassava field, next to a loofah shed, or behind a big tree near the field to hide. In fact, generally speaking, herding cattle is a very happy and comfortable time. The field is lush with greenery, birds chirping, butterflies flying, and roadsides are full of colorful wild flowers. Children can even put down the ox rope and let it freely shuttle back and forth on the grassland without worrying that it will escape.

A gadfly is several times larger than an ordinary fly. As long as one is stopped on the buffalo, it will quickly be surrounded by flies and suck blood together. They will squeeze together and become a dark mass, always sucking until they forget themselves. I just need to make a sound of 'ah -' give a warning to the water buffalo, and then with a single pat, I can always kill a lot of such bad things. Therefore, every time I go to herd cattle, except for holding a book in one hand, my other palm is stained red with buffalo blood. If I'm lucky enough, during the cattle herding process, a blackbird stops on the back of the buffalo, patrols up and down, and pecks at the gadflies, it can also be considered a great help for me. Strange to say, I have found that buffalos that are working (including pulling carts and plowing) are never bitten by gadflies, while buffalos that graze and eat grass will soon attract a large number of gadflies.

As long as there are no classes in school, we will go to the fields to help, at the same time, we will make our work more interesting. For example, when helping cassava pull out the weeds on the ground, my sisters and I, each assigned to self's own row, squatted side by side and moved forward. We used two hands to pull the grass, and the speed was incredibly fast because we inherited our father's work style. If the progress of pulling grass falls behind slightly, the person next to you will reach out to help pull some. We will tug at each other with songs. First, we each think of a song in self's heart, and then we say, "Ready, sing." Everyone sings at the same time, singing self's own song. After a while, some people are not paying enough attention, leading to not knowing what they are humming and singing, and that person can't help but laugh awkwardly.

Snails usually like to eat the leaves or tender buds of crops, which poses a serious threat to crop harvest. Therefore, whenever the rain stops and snails come out to wander around, adults and children always carry buckets of different sizes and walk around every corner of the field to pick up the snails, boil them, and feed them to the ducks. When picking up snails, looking up at the sky, a rainbow hangs high in half of the sky, breathtaking in beauty; Many majestic green cicadas adorned with golden threads on the trees, singing their marching songs sharply, resounding throughout the village, making me feel extremely joyful and uplifted. However, often my fourth sister was full of energy, throwing one after another into the bucket, and my eyesight and hands and feet speed were not as good as hers. Occasionally, I would inevitably stand in place and complain, "Sister, your eyes are as big as those bulls' eyes."

When I was in elementary school, my second sister taught me, "Whenever you hear father or mother call you, you should immediately appear in front of them and ask them what they want." She would do this herself, and I firmly remember these teachings, and I have done the same since then. My parents must have felt this deeply because both my sister and I were able to pass their every test, which made my parents feel very satisfied from the bottom of their hearts.

I have great respect and love for my second sister, who has given me a lot of guidance. When she listened to the teacher's teaching in junior high school, she often relayed it to me. For example, in *The Book of Changes*, there is a saying that emphasizes: caution must be thorough, just like a little fox crossing a river almost successfully, but accidentally wetting its tail, which is unprofitable. She paraphrased what her teacher had said: "There was a child who always said bad things. His father was afraid to hear him say bad things again, so he didn't plan to take him to someone else's wedding. The child begged hard and said, 'I will improve, I promise not to say bad things again. Take me, okay!'" The child participated in the wedding, and indeed kept his mouth tightly closed from beginning to end. His father breathed a sigh of relief, and think he performed really well. As he was about to bid farewell to his master, the child said, "Today, I didn't say a bad word. If anything happens to anyone after we leave, it will have nothing to do with me."

In the past, there were many children in the countryside, and there were five large classes in each grade of Minggang Elementary School. My second sister was admitted to Sanguang Junior High School, but she was the only girl in the entire Luming Village who attended junior high school. All other girls who finished elementary school would not be promoted to middle school, which shows a serious urban-rural gap. Only a few male students apply for junior high school. My home is 7.5 kilometers away from Sanguang Junior High School, and it is a bumpy stone road with no buses to take. The boys in the village always ride bicycles to school, while my second sister has to walk alone before dawn. Whether it's sunny or rainy, she must rush at the fastest pace to arrive at the school before 7:30am. She worked hard and successfully through the harsh test of walking to school during those three years. After graduating from junior high school, she did not apply for high school because no one in the countryside trained girls to pursue such a high degree. Her teachers felt extremely sorry for her.

Later, my second sister signed up for the National Public Service Recruitment Examination, and she passed the exam, working at the Nantou County Tax Office. One day, her supervisor was surprised and asked her, "Do you really only graduate from junior high school? Why did you pass the exam? Others can't even pass the exam even after graduating from university!" Later, my fourth sister encountered a nine-year national compulsory education, and more people finished high school. After graduating from high school, my fourth elder sister successfully entered the winery of the Tobacco and Alcohol

Sales Bureau to work. Considering the remote villages at that time, that was also an admirable strength.

5. Feng Shui and Family Luck

When I was in elementary school, one summer vacation after noon, my father's elder brother's son (my younger cousin) and I were playing by Hulu Pond. Unexpectedly, we were beckoned to ride on Er Bo's ox cart, with at least 5 members of Er Bo's family sitting on the cart. With so many people and so kind greetings, I am preparing to go to a distant and unfamiliar place, towards the direction of "Buxia Village" and a bit close to the foot of Hengshan Mountain, which is clearly beyond the scope of Luming Village; That was a fresh experience I had never had before, and my heart was filled with curiosity and joy.

Everyone arrived at Er Bo's field. Firstly, they quickly plowed rows of sweet potatoes out of the ground. The next step is for the ox cart to slowly move forward, and the people next to the cart quickly throw the sweet potatoes onto the cart. We are responsible for throwing the sweet potatoes up, while someone else on the cart is responsible for receiving them; For me, who is usually active, this is too interesting; Besides, they keep praising us for how great we have performed: "You guys did a great job, full marks."

That evening, when I returned home, it was dark, so dark that I couldn't recognize faces, and I found the atmosphere at home was extremely serious. After a while, my parents came back from outside, and my mother hurried in and loudly asked me where I had gone, as if going crazy. She said she spent half an afternoon running through all the high and low fields of Luming Village, almost shouting her throat out, but couldn't find me. I said that my cousin and I were taken to the field at the foot of the mountain by Er Bo's family. My father closed his eyes slightly and couldn't say a word. It was extremely weird. Time and air seem to stop, as if everyone had forgotten that we hadn't eaten dinner, perhaps we hadn't cooked it yet.

After a while, my mother calmed down and examined the "hanging neck money" hanging from my neck on my chest and hidden in my clothes. It was a protective treasure that was passed through the middle of the "Daoguang Tongbao" ancient coin with thick red thread. It was obtained from the Jintian Temple. I was told by my mother since childhood, "Guanyin Bodhisattva recognizes you as an adopted son and must hang this 'hanging neck money' well on you." Then, my mother said with a little sadness: "When we were in the old house, our sow was about to give birth to piglets, but it died with a red soil footprint on its belly. We dare not live with them again." I only realized the seriousness of the matter at this moment. I was too naive before, which made my parents worry. I decided not to let this kind of thing happen again in the future.

Er Bo has six daughters, two of whom are younger than me, and the older one is very sweet and smart, she is the favorite of Er Bo. However, for some unknown reason, she suffered from mental illness in the fifth grade of elementary school without any reason. Er Bo put in great effort to take her to see doctors, but it was completely ineffective. So, the villagers initiated a joint prayer ceremony for her, inviting the statue of Guanyin from Jintian Temple to his front yard. Every household brought food to worship Guanyin, and the shamans performed magic tricks to ward off her demons. This ceremony was performed twice, but there was no improvement. Later, upon the advice of certain Christians, they converted to Christianity, hoping that the Lord Jesus could cure her illness.

There is a boy in Sanguang Junior High School who is one year older than me and lives in Songbai Ridge. He is the most outstanding boy in the

entire grade. Almost all the teachers and students in the school know him, and the teachers speculate that he is likely to be admitted to the first-choice high school. One day, he suddenly came all the way from Songbai Ridge to visit my home and discussed with my father in the living room. He said he was a Christian and visited my younger cousin in the hospital. He said that my younger cousin mentioned my name to him as if she really wanted to see me; And when she speaks, her smile is beautiful and her eyes are completely normal. Therefore, he believes that if he takes me to talk to her, her illness may improve.

My father frowned and said, "He doesn't understand medicine, he's young, and medical care is a doctor's profession. It's not convenient for us to intervene in this matter." As I was about to say a few good words for my senior, my father impatiently and unreasonably refused, as if everything else was easy to say. No matter how much I tried to persuade him about this matter, he wouldn't listen and allow it. My father also said to him, "Students should study hard. You are a junior high school student and will soon take the entrance exam. Reading is your duty. Don't interfere in such matters that belong to adults." After spending a lot of time talking around, all of these words were the same. Anyway, he just won't let me visit her. My senior had to admit that his lobbying had failed, and with a frustrated expression, he stood up to bid farewell. I walked him for a while, almost to the vicinity of Hulu Pond, before saying goodbye and returning home. As soon as I stepped into the front yard, my father stood in the hallway, still angry and scolding me loudly: "Do children need to intervene in this kind of thing?" I said, "He is the best student in the whole grade, let's not be impolite to him." "What topic is he here to talk about? If you don't listen, go to church with him to listen to 'reason'." My father turned his head in anger and walked into the room.

My second elder male cousin has achieved good grades since childhood.

As he grew up, he not only achieved success in mechanical engineering in the northern region, but also excelled in the study of feng shui geography. He also opened a business to help others watch feng shui. He has a great eloquence and is often entrusted as the host of weddings, funerals, and celebrations. He occasionally returns to his hometown of Luming and drives a Benz car for transportation. Er Bo's children have complained to my father more than once: "There is a problem with the feng shui in the tombs of our ancestors, which benefits only one side and cannot benefit all our descendants." My father never expresses any opinions about these doubts, but our ancestral graves have been relocated one by one under the planning of Er Bo's son, and all auspicious days, locations, directions, and so on are at his discretion. All we can do is repeatedly being notified of the amount to be shared and paying the money.

Er Bo has a daughter who is in the same class as me. I attended Changhua High School and she attended the Night Department of Nantou High School. Her personality is gentle and honest, but she cannot be loved by her father. She goes to work in the field early in the morning and also in the afternoon. It is not until dusk that she hurries off to school and takes the hourly bus to school. After a day of work, she almost ran out of energy; Quiet and honest personality, often late for class; The teacher may not be aware of her life situation, it is said that she always lacks the care of the teacher. High school girls may want to dress up and beautify themselves. She once secretly bought cosmetics and lipstick, applied them on her face, but was beaten by her father, and even cried while crawling, hiding in a dark corner. After a few years, she couldn't bear the hardships and ultimately committed suicide by throwing herself into Hulu Pond.

Since childhood, Er Bo has been bullying the two most loyal and honest siblings - my father and little aunt. Later, he also treated the most loyal daughter among his own children harshly, to the point where she lost her life. I think we have the opportunity to meet or get along with loyal and honest

people in life, which is a test given by heaven to evaluate our conscience score. However, there are indeed many people who cannot pass the tests and ratings of heaven. Is the theory of auspicious or inauspicious feng shui necessarily effective? It is roughly said that if the sum of feng shui score and conscience score is qualified, the so-called auspicious will be effective; Otherwise, can incompetent gods still be called gods?

6. Experience the supernatural

My father has always been very healthy, but unfortunately, a serious illness knocked him down and he only lived to be 84 years old. When he was lying in bed, the doctor had already predicted that he could not be saved. We could only privately request the doctor, "Do not let him suffer at all, because he is a great benevolent person who works hard for a lifetime, and there should not be a painful old age." The doctor agreed. Sometimes, in order to make my father feel comfortable, I use a wheelchair to push him around in the Carrefour Mall in Nantou. I dare not pass the mirror or the glass, because I cried when I strolled around. During my time in the hospital, I often asked, "Do you feel pain?" He always said, "No." I comforted him, "The doctor promised to do his best to help you heal. You can rest assured."

Sometimes, it may be due to medication, and the content of my father's words on the hospital bed seems to go back to his childhood. He becomes very fond of crying and keeps saying, "I want to see my aunt, she loved me the most when I was a child." I don't know what to do, because I have never heard of such a thing, and I don't even know there is such a grandaunt. Such a grandaunt must have grown up in the area near the exit of the Eighteen Bend Ancient Road on the upper side of Luming when she was a child. Her surname was Chen, because my grandmother married from there to the Lin family on the lower side of the village. My third sister heard about this and said, "It is said that when dad was a child, his aunt loved him very much. Later, she married to Changhua County down the mountain. We have no way to find out now." This grandaunt must have passed away already, and I really can't let my father achieve this very special wish during his critical illness. It's a bit regrettable.

One day, my elder granduncle's grandson came to visit my father at his bedside. This elder cousin had a successful career in society and served as the principal of a junior high school. His son is studying at the Medical School of National Taiwan University. My father shouted weakly and painstakingly, sounding as if he was crying: "Your 'Duosang' used to take the money down the mountain to buy farmland, it was the public money of the big family." My elder cousin didn't say anything in reply. He was silent for a while, just hoping that my father would take care of himself. After that, he hurriedly left.

On the afternoon of January 16th, 2007, I returned from Taipei to Nantou Hospital and walked into the ward. My father saw me, his face was full of smiles, and I also smiled. The foreign caregiver saw us laughing so happily, standing in the corner, smiling slightly, too. Unexpectedly, that night, I received a call from my younger sister saying that my father had passed away. I hurried home. My younger sister said, "In the evening, Dad asked us to use a wheelchair to push him to the front of the hospital's Buddha hall. He held up his hand and said, 'Amitabha Buddha, Amitabha Buddha.' He said it several times. Unexpectedly, after a while, the injection could not enter his body and stopped. We immediately notified the doctor, who announced that he had passed away." It was a peaceful passing.

As soon as the news of my father's passing was announced, Er Bo's second son (my second elder male cousin) came to my living room, along with other brothers from the same clan who came to help out voluntarily. My second elder male cousin, who also works as a feng shui watcher in the north,

is considered an expert. My second younger uncle who lives across the courtyard recommends my second elder male cousin to take on the planning work for my father's funeral, including selecting a day, arranging funeral ceremonies, selecting the location of the bone tower. I think, after all, it's my father's nephew who helped my father, so there should be no problem. Therefore, I immediately agreed to entrust my second elder male cousin with arranging the funeral plan. Anyway, we will pay the "gift money for the day planner" according to the regulations. My second elder male cousin asked me to provide the birthdays, months, and years of the relevant people. I flipped through the notebook and answered any questions and provided him with the relevant data on the spot.

On the evening of January 19th, my mother suddenly ran to the courtyard and cried loudly in front of my father's spiritual table, because she only then realized that the person who helped my father watch feng shui and choose a day was my second elder male cousin. My mother scolded me and said, "Why did you entrust him to mark the funeral? Don't you know how much we suffered and how much bullying we suffered back then?"

"I'm not unaware. It was recommended by my second younger uncle, and my second elder male cousin also agreed to help on the spot. I could not refuse the recommendation. Moreover, we are all our own people, and there shouldn't be any problems. This time, we'll choose to trust him, okay?" I was originally trying to prevent my mother from being overly sad. I generally did not discuss my father's funeral arrangements with her, but I just hoped that my sisters and I would share this important responsibility.

On January 20th, after my second elder male cousin helped my father select a funeral schedule, he wrote a notice paper and pasted it on the wall next to our hall door. It mentioned the day of entering the tower, with a warning of the situation of Chongsha, and wrote: "On the day of entering the tower, people who are not eligible for the age of Gengshen, 27, or 87". On the 12th day of the 12th lunar month, when the coffin was moved, he wrote, "It is not suitable for people who belong to the ox or the chicken." However, on the 14th of December, he wrote, "It is not suitable for the Gengshen." I didn't say anything and immediately gave him a "red envelope of money for the date-selector" to thank him.

On January 22nd, my second elder male cousin took me to the Mingjian Township Office to choose a location for my father in the tower. We walked into the tower where the urns were placed, and he led me around row after row, up and down. After looking it over, we walked into the office to register together, including the serial number and seat orientation.

On January 24th, I had a splitting headache and had to find a leather hat from the wardrobe that could cover my cheeks. Originally, this hat was meant to be burned to my deceased father, but I couldn't care too much. It's important to wear it as a cold protector first. At night, even the eyes began to ache.

My father's mourning hall was entrusted to a funeral company in our hometown to arrange and handle the funeral. After discussing it, we decided to use "Buddhist rituals" for the funeral. There is the highest guardian deity on my father's throne, which is the Earth Treasure King Bodhisattva. 24 hours a day, incense sticks as thick as fingers should be ignited in the incense burner, one after another, without interruption. In addition, it is also necessary to light a few more delicate incense sticks on time every day, devout worship.

At noon on January 25th, my third sister looked flustered and took my hand, walking to the spiritual table. She said, "Come on, do you think this is strange? The incense I lit immediately burned to the bottom as soon as it was inserted into the incense burner."

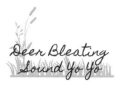

My third sister tried to insert a worship incense, which immediately turned into ashes. This is completely different from the so-called "burning furnace" in the temple. The incense burner in the temple is because the believers have inserted too much incense, and some people believe that it will naturally ignite a large fire in the furnace. The incense burner on my father's spiritual table was almost empty except for the ash powder at the bottom and no other incense feet on top. My third sister lit another incense, and I thought to myself, yes, within 5 seconds, the entire incense burned to ashes, including the red incense feet, leaving no trace of it. My third sister was surprised and said, "How could it be so hot?"

"Yes, why is it so hot?"

At three o'clock in the afternoon, I went shopping in Nantou City, I received a phone call from my younger sister: "Brother, it's too scary! The incense we inserted turned into ashes on the spot. I tried to touch the incense burner and found that the ashes were actually cold. I have already thrown a set of money cups and asked father for instructions. The instructions I received were to change the day planner. I also called our second elder male cousin and said we need to ask someone else to make a different arrangement and choose a new day to enter the tower. He replied on the phone: 'The younger generation must respect the wishes of the elders. Back then, my teacher once told me not to help people in the same village choose auspicious days. '"

I agreed with my younger sister's opinion on the phone and planned to ask another date planner to help us arrange the funeral time. Returning to Luming, my fourth sister also returned home. She carefully examined the announcement paper outside the hall and said, "Isn't your eldest son's zodiac sign a monkey? Monkey is the Shen of the Twelve Earthly Branches. Dad's funeral will be held on the day of hurting Shen. Isn't that hurting the eldest grandson? He didn't write about harming monkeys, but he wrote about harming Shen. As for December 12th, the taboo when moving the coffin is: 'It's not suitable for people born in the Year of the Ox to be present.' Our younger sister is born in the Year of the Ox. What kind of conspiracy is this situation?" Fortunately, my fourth sister once took a course in "*The Book of Changes*" at a community university, I used to reject those theories of Yin and Yang, Feng Shui, and fortune telling from my mind. I completely ignored this knowledge. As a result, I fell into such a dangerous situation without realizing it. I was so frightened that I broke out in a cold sweat and blamed myself endlessly.

On January 26th, I followed another expert who helped us choose an auspicious day and went to the township office.

"I want to change my father's tower position," I said to the staff. "Because I've been having a headache lately, the incense burning on the incense burner on the spiritual table has turned into ashes within 5 seconds. It's strange. Can my father's tower entry date be changed? Because we hired another day selector who chose an auspicious day. How much do we need to pay for it?"

"No need to pay extra charge, we can help you change it. Headache and other issues are common things that we've seen too much. A few days ago, you came to choose a tower location, and after walking out, several colleagues in our office discussed this matter and said, 'Too strange! why did anyone choose this kind tower location to sit in the east and face to the west this year?'"

I was shocked by his explanation and thanked him on the spot. Returning home, my headache unexpectedly healed without any medicine. We announced the hiring of another day selector who will help my father choose another auspicious day. My second elder male cousin quietly refunded the "Sir's gift money" he had previously received from me to my family, and without saying a word, he hastily left.

The general obituary always states at the end that "the family is too numerous to be recorded", as if a statement was made to "not offend others". I don't want to be disrespectful to my clan either. In my father's obituary, I carefully included the names of my father's "nephews" in order to be considered polite. My father's elder brother's early ex-wife gave birth to two sons and a daughter. After the death of the eldest aunt, the wife who remarried gave birth to several more children. The two sons born to the elder Uncle in his early years may have believed that his father had been taken care of by a new woman, so the two brothers moved to settle in Taitung; Always unable to come back frequently to visit relatives and friends in Luming Village. Taitung is indeed far away, but my two elder cousins always inform my father through Er Bo about their marriage, housewarming, and other auspicious events held in Taitung. My father always quickly takes out the congratulatory gift money and entrusts Er Bo to bring it to Taitung and give it to them, without any disrespect. This time it was the news of my father's passing. I inquired about Taitung's phone number and should contacted the two elder cousins in Taitung to inform them that their little uncle had passed away.

But neither of the two elder cousins in Taitung answered the phone in person. I don't know their family members, and during the phone call, they were simply stuttering, vague, and confused, as if they couldn't figure out who the other person was. I am filled with confusion, but I can only let this matter go.

Finally, my father's funeral was successfully completed, and we had no great demands or feng shui intentions, only seeking all peace. On the occasion of my father's funeral ceremony, my elder granduncle's grandson (the cousin who serves as the principal of a junior high school) enthusiastically jumped out as the host and helped my father and my family say a lot of good things on stage.

A few years later, my Er Bo passed away, arranged for a Christian ceremony. I took the time to return to Luming Village and pay respects in front of the spiritual hall, but they did not provide an opportunity to see the remains. On the day of the funeral, I was unable to go to the scene to pay tribute because there were classes at school. Afterwards, my younger sister told me, "On the day of Er Bo's funeral, two elder cousins living in Taitung came back. In the courtyard, when someone introduced me as his little uncle's daughter, he said in front of everyone, 'Since we moved to Taitung, my little uncle has never had any contact with us in terms of gifts or money.' I immediately clarified and said, 'My father has never failed to give gifts and blessings, and the red envelopes are all entrusted to our Er Bo to take to Taitung, which is known to all of our family. My father is the most upright person and has never been impolite to you.'"

The little aunt who married to Tianzi Village is already old and must be supported when walking. Every second day of the first lunar month, she insists on his son taking her back to the mother's house of Luming. It seems that as long as there is still a breath left, she misses the "root" of Luming Village all her life, especially when she comes to the photo of my father hanging on the wall. She always stares at it for a while, which deeply moves me. Once, she said in a solemn tone, "When your Er Bo passed away, his eyes were wide open and couldn't close."

After retiring from her teaching career, my wife became a happy Buddhist believer and often watched Buddhist preaching programs on TV, she once relayed the opinions of the masters: "*Miraculous Lotus Sutra* records that even the bad guy Tebhadata can be predicted to become a Buddha in the future. This is like the drama of life, no matter whether they play good guys or bad guys, every actor gets a salary." She also mentioned the story in the *Diamond*

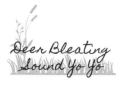

Sutra, saying: "Anything that torments me in daily life can be regarded as King Golly's dismemberment of me. It's better to regard the other side's evil deeds as removing my karma."

In 2015, I encountered another incredible phenomenon resembling a supernatural. Under the recommendation of Professor Li from Fu Ren University, I plan to participate in the "International Symposium on Zhang Huang's Academic Thoughts and the 110th Anniversary of the Birth of Mr. Lu Zongda" and the "Third Anniversary of Mr. Chen Xinxiong's Death and Academic Thoughts Symposium" at Beijing Normal University from August 24th to 26th. I agree to publish two papers:

1.   *"A Case Study of Mr. Ji Gang and His son-in-law Pan Shi Zen's Interaction in "Huang Kan Diary"*

2.   *"The correlation between Mr. Ji Gang's lifestyle and health status in "Huang Kan Diary"*

On March 13th, 2015, as usual, I went to Lin Kou Ding Fu Cemetery to pay tribute to Teacher Pan. That was a trip I would definitely go to before the Qingming Festival every year. This year, both of my upcoming papers are closely related to Professor Pan Zhonggui, as he is Mr. Huang Jigang's son-in-law and a popular figure in "Huang Kan Diary". I mentioned my August itinerary during the worship and asked Teacher Pan to bless me with success.

The strange thing happened on July 20th, because Mr. Zhang Binglin gave the name of Mr.潘重規; Before this, there were several names for Teacher Pan. In the "Huang Kan Diary" by Jiangsu Education Publishing House, page 398 was written as "重奎" and page 571 was written as "崇奎". Suddenly, I noticed this difference and reminded myself to be careful not to make typos. Previously, I had already inputted almost all of Teacher Pan's name and events into the computer. I plan to use the search function to confirm if I am completely correct. The result is that when I input the word '崇奎' and want to 'search', the entire computer screen fades and stops moving; It crashed. I was busy for a while but it didn't work, so I had to press and hold the power button to force it to shut down. When I restarted the computer and entered other words to test the 'search' function, I found that it was functioning normally. However, when I input '崇奎' again and press 'Find', it immediately crashes again. That time was around midnight, and only my light was on in the entire research building. I felt particularly peaceful around me. I couldn't help but shed tears and knelt on both knees, closed my palms, and said, "Teacher, I didn't know you were with me next to me." I forced the computer to shut down, restarted it, and stopped trying again. Later, the computer function was completely normal.

Now, if someone asks me, do gods really exist? I will say, "Although I cannot see the gods with my eyes, I believe it 100%."

7. Things change and stars shift

Luming, a village that had already been cultivated during the Qing Dynasty, was observed from various perspectives after several rounds of human and material relocation. It was like experiencing a changing situation, and the village's appearance was not as good as before.

In ancient times, the stone road dedicated to cattle and sheep that villagers used to lead to Hengshan was widened and filled up. Now, it has become a double track asphalt road for car traffic, and a new passage has been opened from the side of Hengshan to reach the rear of the mountain, leading to Yuanlin; There used to be several shade trees on the Cow and Sheep Road, but now they are all gone.

The pond dedicated to soaking water for buffalo next to Hulu Pond has been diverted and drained because the village's cattle have completely disappeared. It has now been filled and turned into a piece of land for construction.

Due to the impact of modern technological civilization, the attractiveness of the external industry and commerce, as well as the continuous exploitation of agricultural products by merchants, low crop prices, and even insufficient income, young people in Luming Village abandoned their homes and went out to struggle, hoping to find a better way out. The son inherits the father's business, which was praised by the ancients, shows no substantial significance or value advantage here. However, the key factor that truly went against the original intention due to improper handling is the construction of substations.

Things are unpredictable, the sea may become land, and land may become the sea. The northeast corner of Luming used to be a vast countryside, with winding paths intertwined. The banks of the fields are high and low, with big trees, vines, crops, grasslands, mysterious, remote, tranquil and quiet; There are many memories of the labor and growth of villagers there. Later, this large area of rural land disappeared and was expropriated by the government, using bulldozers to destroy and level it. Moreover, it was surrounded by high walls, including a substation and many electric towers that extend outward, as well as densely packed high-voltage wires. Occasionally walking along the wall, attempting to retrieve some memories of the past, but the concern in my heart is not the high-voltage electric waves, but the emotional impact of the scene; To be more practical, it is blocked by a high wall and cannot be seen at all.

The development history of Luming has left a deep impression on the villagers. Looking back on the beautiful rural scenes of the past, in contrast to today's ugly appearance, it is not only the pain of blood and heartache. Villagers all know, what is it called "passing down the firewood"? They stood by the Hulu Pond, imagining the herds of wild deer and the traces of their ancestors during the Qing Dynasty. They also stood by the substation, imagining the countryside, wilderness, and childhood memories. Now they have all become a dream and a passing cloud.

There is no sense of death when cutting the head with a soft knife. When officials and villagers communicated about land acquisition, were there suspicions of misleading the appearance and nature of the substation? Why don't they know how to stand up and protest to defend this pure land? In fact, the villages that have always been closed and loyal villagers simply lack relevant common sense and experience in resistance. Unfortunately, with a vast view, stable terrain, remote land, and cheap prices, it is easy to expropriate. The construction of the substation can only be attributed to the fact that "Mountain trees grow into useful timber and invite the fate of being cut down." The villagers of Luming are now silently bearing the unpleasant consequences ahead of them.

At this point in the construction of the substation, even with the magic of shifting stars, there may be no choice. Now, outsiders driving up and down Hengshan, passing by Luming Village, see that one side of the village is covered with electric towers and wires. If they stop for a short break and take a walk, they would probably feel bored and discouraged! Who would have imagined that it was originally a wilderness where birds and animals to roam and rest, and it was also a paradise for rural children to play and explore? It's a quiet place without the need for official offices, a poetic and picturesque garden, and a window for simple people to converse with heaven.

8. Hope deer come again

"I advise you not to shoot down the birds of spring. The young birds are in their nests hoping for the return of the mother bird." If the children who

grazed cattle and sheep in the past grew up in today's environment that emphasizes ecological protection, or if the people's livelihood and economy were not so difficult, perhaps there would not be so many birds, beasts, insects, etc. being persecuted by people. In recent years, groups of macaques have been protected on the Fengbai hiking trail between Ershui and Songbai Ridge; It is said that until the Qing Dynasty, there were still many deer in the area of Lukuit, but now all of them have disappeared.

In the summer of 2004, when I was walking alone on the slope of the Chengde Summer Resort, my mind was full of imagination about the possible summer vacation for members of the Qing Dynasty royal family. Suddenly, a few wild deer walked out of the forest in front of me, and I stared for half a day; They are so gentle and leisurely, so familiar and friendly! It is said that during the Qing Dynasty, there were many wild deer in my hometown Lukuit under the forest. Isn't it like this?

Su Dongpo said, "Things are like a spring dream, after which there is no trace." It is best not to turn the story of Lu Ming into nothing like a spring dream. It is a living struggle history of the people since the end of the Qing Dynasty. Luming was once the endpoint of the Eighteen Bend Ancient Salt Road, a place for merchants and porters to breathe a sigh of relief. It was a land of abundant forests and grass, thick soil, and simple people. Flowers, plants, and trees have their own meaning in existence, why ask beauty to come and take them? The villagers, with a humble heart and sincere thoughts, only pay attention to the true colors of their village; Everyone is calm and self-sufficient, contented and always happy. It is not possible to produce rare treasures here. As long as there is a small space for the villagers to live in, they feel at ease. Although the history of the development and evolution of this ancient village in the past was ordinary and tranquil, it also had a strong sense of antiquity, and its nostalgic value and status were enough to compete with the bustling cities.

The landscape in the northeast corner of the village has been destroyed by a large substation, but other areas of the village are still in good condition. In recent years, with the advancement of leisure concepts, Luming and surrounding scenic spots have been connected. Tourists walk from Qingshui Rock to the top of the Eighteen Bend Ancient Salt Road, and the cool breeze under the pavilion is gentle, giving them a refreshing feeling; To the west, you can overlook the scenery of Changhua County, as far as the seaside; Looking eastward at the numerous majestic mountains of Nantou County. And Luming itself is a village that evokes nostalgia for the past. Tourists can also walk along the bike path from Qingshui Rock to Hengshan Cliff, the Northwest Angle of Luming. During the spring equinox season every year, in conjunction with the eagle watching activities in the Bagua Mountains, standing on the edge of Luming Village and overlooking the foot of the mountain, one can see the heroic posture of eagles soaring in the sky.

"I remember that I was a young man who once rode a bamboo horse, but in a blink of an eye I became a white-headed man." From the perspective of eternity and billions of years, this short story of Luming Village is as fleeting as a blink of an eye; I personally reminisce about the past and try to create literary works for it, trying to capture that fleeting moment of time and not let it disappear with the passage of time; Although it is just cherishing one's own old broom, it can express one's love for one's hometown. We sincerely express our gratitude and nostalgia for Luming's ancestors who did not fear the cold and heat, sacrificed their blood and sweat, and established a simple and beautiful folk custom.

Let the deer reappear! This is my earnest wish, which may contain certain meanings and reasons. Therefore, I have written an article titled '*Looking forward to the deer bleating again*':

This place first had a cluster of wild deer, and later became known as the 'Lukuit'. Deers have the virtue of calling out when they see their food, and later villages are called 'Luming'. Deer is actually the owner of this place, and humans are just guests. It has been a long time, the phenomenon of unreasonable guest noise overwhelming the owner's voice.

From Shetou Township in Changhua, slowly climbing up the mountains, the lush forests allow you to roam freely. The villages on the mountains are quaint and elegant, and human nature is sublimated. They have learned not to engage in hunting anymore. The water in Hulu Pond is still clear, and the villagers welcome the deer babies to gather again and enjoy the joy of family life at any time.

The artist's ingenious idea is to draw bats to symbolize blessings, and to shape deer to symbolize wealth. Deer is an auspicious fairy beast, and people in Luming Village need deer in their daily lives to accompany and bless them. Roughly speaking, deer have four main symbols and are worth striving for:

Firstly, Symbolizing the spirit of active participation in the world –"Luming Feast (Deer Bleating Feast)":

The Book of Songs records: "With pleased sounds the deer call to one another, eating the celery of the fields. I have here admirable guests; the lutes are struck, and the organ is blown." "I have good wine, to feast and make glad the hearts of my admirable guests." The Tang Dynasty held a banquet for the new imperial examination, and the Song Dynasty held a banquet for the top scorers in the literary and military examinations, both known as the "Luming Feast (Deer Bleating Feast)". It encourages new members of the officialdom to actively pursue their aspirations and proclaims that the work of serving the country and society is about to be promoted and put into practice.

Secondly, the secluded place of the elite – "Lumen Mountain":

Pang Degong of the Eastern Han Dynasty once praised Zhuge Liang as the "Crouching Dragon", Pang Tong as the "Phoenix Child", and Sima Hui as the

"Water Mirror", known as the "Wisdom of Knowing People". Such an expert lives a leisurely and self-satisfied life, living in seclusion in Lumen Mountain. Ming Dynasty Chen Jiru said, "After Huang Shigong subdued Zhang Liang, he lived in seclusion in Gucheng; After conquering Kong Ming, Pang Degong lived in seclusion in Lumen Mountain, while Lao Tzu lived in seclusion in the desert after conquering Confucius. These three people all had the situation of 'success and retirement'."

Thirdly, can strengthen one's physical fitness – deer play:

Huatuo Wuqinxi, featuring tigers, deer, bears, apes, and birds; Tigers value strength, deer value comfort, bears value stability, apes value agility, and birds value lightness. The practice of deer play is to support the ground with all four limbs, turn your neck and look back, three times to the left and two times to the right, extend your feet left and right, and also stretch and retract three times to the left and two times to the right. When feeling unwell, getting up and engaging in one of the five movements of the Huatuo will make you sweat freely, making your body feel refreshed and craving for food increase greatly. Wu Pu, a student of Huatuo, practiced this sport and lived for over ninety years. He had intelligent ears and eyes, and his teeth were firm.

Fourth, the Holy Land for Buddhahood – Deer Park:

In 531 BC, after becoming a Buddha, Sakyamuni came to Deer Park (Sarnath) to discuss the Four Noble Truths in detail, and passed five monks, including Kauchenru; By this time, the three treasures of Buddhism, namely Buddha, Dharma, and Monk, had been established and completed. Therefore, "Deer Park (Sarnath)" has become a memorial site for the Buddha's first turn to Falun, and one of the four holy places of Buddhism.

We all love deer, and we also love the four major aspects of deer symbolism. We sincerely hope that the wild deer will reappear and bring us happiness and joy!

18 Bend Ancient Road

At the top of the Eighteen Bend Ancient Salt Road - The Land Temple (the
Tudigong Temple) of Lu Ming

Overlooking Changhua County from Luming

Looking at the cliff of Hengshan from the top of the ancient salt road.

Hulu Pond

Jintian Temple

Lu Ming - Lin Family Ancient House

The Sanheyuan where the author moved in at the age of three

The Jintian Temple archway next to Hulu Pond

Luming and Hengshan

Substation

The newly opened road passes through the Acacia forest in Hengshan

9. The spirit of hard work

No matter how the external environment changes, rural people have their own genes for striving for excellence, and their simple and loyal qualities make them more likely to accept good education.

People with lofty ideals in ancient times believed that a more ideal life is to avoid "people rot like vegetation", although this ideal was very difficult to achieve! But it is still worth our lifelong self encouragement and dedication.

I think one of my research achievements is the world's number one, which makes me feel a little relieved. Professor Wang Li from Beijing University and Professor Chen Xinxiong from Taiwan Normal University are two major authorities in phonology. My ancient phonetics comes from Professor Chen's teachings. His "*Collection of Studies on Diligent and unremitting Study*" records that when he read Li Daoyuan's "*Annotations on the Water Classics*", he discovered a phenomenon that he could not understand. He raised questions and also indicated that this was a problem that he could not solve. So, I put in a lot of effort to study and finally solved his confusion. Later, I received a letter from Teacher Chen expressing praise and affirmation; This is what is called 'my world number one'.

The above-mentioned problem refers to a peculiar phenomenon hidden in academic materials, here are a few brief examples:

1. There is a sentence in *The Book of Changes* that reads "其文蔚也", and the version of *The Book of Changes* cited in "*Shuowen Jiezi*" is written as "其文斐也".

2. The silk version of *The Book of Changes* in Mawangdui has a term for '洫若', while the commonly used version of *The Book of Changes* is written as '發若'.

3. The book '*Erya*' contains the term '鼩鼠'. *The Classic Commentary* states: "The character '鼩' is written in some versions as '蚡', and this character also has a pronunciation of '偃'. *Guangya* records that 鼩鼠 is 鼱鼠."

4. In the book "*Xunzi*", there is a term for "芬薌", and in the same situation, "*Han Shi Waizhuan*" is written as "芬芳".

5. In the book "*The Spring and Autumn Annals of the Lu Family*", the term "非濱之東" is widely recognized by the academic community as "渭濱之東", and there is a rule of "borrowing".

6. The term "子帝槐立" in the book "*Shiji*" is written as "子帝芬立" in other versions.

7. In the book "*Shiji*", the term "其政乖" is written in other versions as "其政煩".

8. In the book "*The Book of Han*", the sentence "鷃雀飛集丞相府" is written in other versions as "鳲雀飛集丞相府".

9. In the book '*Huainanzi*', the term '多懼害勇' is used. In other versions, it is written as '多懼妨勇'.

10. There are strange words such as "思任發" and "思卜發" in the book "*Ming Shi*", which should be changed to "思任王" or "思卜王". This is purely a misrecording phenomenon by historians in "*Ming Shi*".

No one in the academic community had ever dealt with this issue, and no one had ever given an answer. In 2018, I went to Beijing Normal University to give a speech, which was to introduce the research process and results to them. After solving this problem, we can correct the famous law of Qian Daxin of the Qing Dynasty, which states that "the light lipped sound belongs to the heavy lipped sound in ancient times". Although these research results are inevitably boring and uninteresting for the general public, there is always

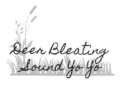

someone to take care of academic issues in the field of expertise. No matter how boring and uninteresting it is, I must explore it seriously and patiently. Afterwards, in the history of phonological research, it is necessary for the academic community to mention my achievement. My paper on this topic was published in the seventh issue of "*Journal of Literature* at Nanhua University: *New Keys to Literature*". It is also included in my book "*Collection of Exploratory Works on Chinese Studies*", and there is no need to elaborate on it here.

Beijing Normal University

In 2018, I gave a speech at Beijing Normal University, with Director Qi Yuantao on the right.

In addition, Tai Chi Chuan is my favorite sport. Since 1977, I have been practicing Tai Chi Chuan under the guidance of Teacher Wu Guozhong, who was the high-footed disciple of the late Teacher Zheng Manqing. Later on, I entered the workplace to teach and temporarily stopped practicing Tai Chi Chuan due to my busy schedule. Later, when I arrived in Central Taiwan, I joined Professor Ye Wenkuan's team and continued to learn Tai Chi; Teacher Ye is currently the chairman of the Tai Chi Chuan Federation of the Republic of China. I feel that having the opportunity to practice Tai Chi Chuan is my great fortune. Of course, only those with profound personal experience can be so sincerely convinced. Later, I went to Beijing University twice to publish papers and served as the host of a Tai Chi Academic Seminar; On this occasion, I was on the same stage as my third son, which was quite interesting. Keep working hard, in the future!

Old Gate of Beijing University

Beijing University hosted a Tai Chi Chuan academic seminar, and I served as the host.

Part 2

Behold A Rainbow

During my master's program, I was on the top floor of the Dazhuang Hall at the University of Chinese Culture

Chapter 1　Listening to the speech and meeting Feng Qing

One day during my first year of my master's degree, I learned from a poster on the wall that The Young Women's Association of the School would hold a series of "Love and Marriage" speeches, which would be divided into three nights.

On the first day, Professor Yang will give a lecture on the topic of "Who will spend the golden years with - friendship, love". The speech hasn't started yet, all the seats are occupied. The students continued to rush in, and around the classroom, there were all standing students, crowded to the brim.

Professor Yang walked into the classroom and received enthusiastic applause. The host finished his introduction and the speech began. At this moment, two or three girls walked in together. They had already occupied their seats with backpacks, which was in the center of the front row. Several classmates and I crowded next to Professor Yang, and I found the only foothold in front of the blackboard, facing all the seats.

Among the girls who just came in, one immediately caught my eye. She was wearing long pants and looked simply. Upon hearing some funny things, I couldn't help but watch her smile. Oddly enough, it seems that she also took this opportunity to watch me smile. She has a pair of bright eyes and sparkling white teeth, making her look lively and energetic; I try to look around and feel that the brightness of a hundred stars is not as bright as the light of a moon.

After two hours, the speech ended. Professor Yang was about to step down and bow, but she rushed out of the classroom and ran without a trace.

The next day's speech, titled "Between the eyebrows and in the heart, there is no way to avoid - the interaction between men and women" was delivered by a young Dr. Mou. I went to the venue early to take a seat, flipped through a book, and sat quietly waiting.

The crowd gradually surged in, and the beautiful woman I saw yesterday did indeed appear again. She was wearing a golden dress, which was even more eye-catching than the previous time. She helped with the chores at the meeting, prepared tea, and activated the loudspeaker, which made me realize that she was a member of the organizing unit.

When Dr. Mou spoke, she sat in the middle of the classroom. At the end of the speech, the beautiful woman's behavior was the same as last time. Amidst thunderous applause, the chairman had not yet delivered a thank-you speech. She left her seat first and quickly walked out of the classroom.

Returning to my dormitory, I felt disappointed and lost. Firstly, I didn't know her name, and secondly, I heard Dr. Mu's opinion, as if men in society are likely to have an affair; Is it true that men are so shallow and unreliable in terms of emotional dedication? Why do humans sing the supreme value of love, saying one thing and doing another? Is it really so difficult for men and women to know each other and cherish each other, insisting on pure and steadfast love?

The third lecture in the series will be led by Professor Zhu. In order to see her, I deliberately didn't occupy a seat. At the beginning of the speech, there were no more available seats, so I stood in front of the classroom with a group of people to listen. However, I can confirm that she did not attend the lecture.

After returning to the dormitory, I lay on the table and wanted to take a nap, but couldn't fall asleep. I had to pick up a ballpoint pen and jot down a few of the speeches I had heard in the past few days, except for Dr. Mu:

(1) What is the difference between "love" and "like"?

Love must possess several major characteristics: 1. eye contact. 2. Exclusivity, which means unwillingness to have a third-party present. 3. Forget about the environment, because of this, there are professional pickpockets in the park who specialize in stealing men's and women's handbags. 4. Promote the good of the other party and conceal their evil. 5. Unable to keep it confidential, willing to say anything. 6. Love my house and love my dog. Finally, it should be noted that these Romantic phenomena of "love" do not last forever, they occur at a certain stage.

(2) Is there any "friendship" between men and women?

It can exist, but male physiology is unique, in addition to "love" and "like", there is also a keen sexual desire; This special instinct is different from that of women, it is bestowed by God; Only in this way can the race continue to exist. As long as men accept moral norms and overcome the third instinct, "friendship" between men and women can exist.

(3) What are the important differences in sexual psychology between men and women?

The situation for men is: "If he gets it, he wants to give it up." The situation for women is: "If she gets it, she wants to have it." The former is reproductive, allowing the race to continue; The latter is maternal, so the next generation can receive good protection and upbringing, and humanity has always praised her as "the great mother". Men's characteristics have positive functions, but they are also a "despicable trait"; If you ask men in the world: "Who is your ideal spouse?" they will always answer: "The one I haven't met yet." Since there are the above negative situations, we realize the importance of moral cultivation. Only by relying on moral constraints can men and women avoid many unfortunate events and live a life of cherishing blessings and happiness.

(4) Can girls take the initiative?

Without him realizing it, you can try to take the initiative, such as dropping a handkerchief, letting him to help you pick it up, and so on.

(5) The people I like don't come to me, but the people I don't like come to me. I completely refuse them, is that okay?

No way. Why don't you "ride a donkey to find a horse"? You can get along with them lightly, and you cannot lack them; Because most people dare not make a friend who is "nobody wants to pursue". If there is a group of suitors around, it may attract more suitors.

(6) How to choose a reliable spouse?

If you want to choose a girl, you must look at her family upbringing. Because first-class mothers will teach first-class daughters. When choosing a boy, observe whether he is filial; Because if a man is not filial, he is often not a man who can sincerely love his wife.

(7) At what age is it ideal to start searching for friends of the opposite sex?

When will you encounter your ideal partner? It should be "Suiyuan" (follow fate), as you may also encounter good childhood sweethearts when you are young. But there is a phenomenon that must be referred to, as the Taiwanese proverb goes: "The big chicken crows later." Chicken breeders all know that some of the same batch of chicks quickly enter puberty, with bright feathers and a majestic appearance, and soon begin to crow. We can categorically say, "They have a small physique" because they stop growing when they are small and will stay with this physique throughout their lives. At this time, some companions were completely bald, with sparse feathers and no luster, only focused on feeding. This was actually an "awe inspiring" chicken, which could later turn into a massive rooster. Therefore, if middle

school students or high school students fall in love or try forbidden fruits, their future achievements will often be lower.

Chapter 2   Discovery

The speech activity has come to an end, and I am eager to find out about the beautiful woman I have met twice before. Firstly, I called The Young Women's Association of the School to inquire, and they said they couldn't help me. I asked my junior sister from the literature department to borrow activity photos from The Young Women's Association on my behalf, but she also failed to borrow them; The response from the Director General of The Young Women's Association to my junior sister was: "In that speech, those sitting in the first row were all teachers; if they were students, we would all know each other." In that case, the investigation work had to be suspended, and I was still full of doubts.

One day, after class, I walked past the dance classroom and suddenly realized that "she" was "she". She was standing inside the dance classroom. Although the door was closed, through the glass, it was still certain that it was her; I was refreshed.

The bottom half of the glass is covered by wooden boards. I slowly moved my steps, climbed halfway up the stairs, and observed from a distance; I'll come down later and go up again later. I've done these three times. The students are still scattered and unable to form a team; Some talk, some do warm-up exercises. Two more girls came outside the door, placed their shoes in the cabinet outside, and then walked into the classroom.

I stopped in the middle of the stairs and stared at the small piece of glass above the dance classroom. I noticed that she was looking straight ahead, full of energy, watching the mirror by the wall twisting her hips quickly and fiercely, and then laughing happily on her own. I was startled and said, "Oh my goodness! Such lively and rough movements!"

The class started, but after all, the vision was too narrow, and the dancers were quite far away from one another. When everyone danced, I couldn't see if she was also dancing; When I saw her jump, I wasn't sure if anyone else was jumping. I am puzzled whether she is a teacher or a student. So, I went outside the office of the dance department to check the class schedule and found that this class has Chinese language class in the afternoon.

At three o'clock in the afternoon, I walked to the Chinese language classroom. Surprisingly, it was finally confirmed that she was a student. Before the teacher arrived, she was talking to another girl and accidentally turned her head. When she saw me standing outside the back door, she immediately turned back and remained silent.

This class is their midterm exam, and I am outside the classroom, sometimes far away, sometimes close. "What should I do when she comes out later?" I thought and walked towards the far corner, waiting.

She finally appeared, standing outside the classroom talking with several classmates, holding a stick in her hand and spinning a circle. Soon, her three classmates walked towards the bathroom, and I turned around, slightly avoiding them; Until they came out of the restroom and walked back to their original position. Just a moment later, she walked alone towards the direction of the restroom, and I was secretly pleased and temporarily avoided it; It wasn't until she walked out that I bowed forward and said:

"I am a first-year student in the master's program at the Institute of Literature. I have seen you twice."

"Really? Where did you see me?"

"When listening to a speech about making friends."

"Are you an overseas Chinese?"

"No, I'm from Taiwan. What's the matter? Is the tone different?"

I saw her not answering, and then said, "My name is Wang Wang. What about you?"

"My name is Feng Qing."

We looked at each other and I said, "I noticed you!".

"……" Feng Qing smiled slightly and said, "My classmates are waiting for me over there. Let's talk about it later."

"Goodbye."

"Goodbye."

Feng Qing quickly walked towards her classmates, as delicate as a beautiful fairy; I stared blankly and felt very happy in my heart.

Chapter 3   First Date

Having already known Feng Qing's name, I wrote a letter that night and placed it in the dance department mailbox outside the school's mail room.

April 17, 1982

Dear Feng Qing:

Yesterday, a few words were not only an honor; Your extraordinary appearance is considered pleasing to the eye, triggering my sensitive heart. I believe you must be extremely self cherishing. I don't know how to describe you, just say 'goddess'.

Please believe that if no one had appreciated me before, I wouldn't dare to expect you to appreciate me today. I have my perseverance and stubbornness in pursuit of my "ideal". How many hesitations, how many troubles, how many nightmares, I used to feel like God was playing tricks on me.

I have the strictest self-discipline, and I have never even attended a ball, just to get a good girl who completely falls in love with her. And I admit that I am not a conservative and stubborn scholar. Who doesn't love the beauty of art? Therefore, measuring the field of study that you and I have, I believe that this friendship between us should not be impossible.

The "realistic me" is dirty, filthy, greedy, and cruel, but the "conscience me" is pure as jade. I like the British poet William Wordsworth's "Rainbow Poems", roughly as follows:

My heart leaps up when I behold
A rainbow in the sky;
So was it, when my life began;
So is it now I am a man;
So be it when I shall grow old,
Or let me die!

The British poet Emerson said, "A pure soul is the most precious thing in the world." To preserve innocence and purity forever would be a shining and immortal heart; I will encourage myself with this.

"The cloud wishes to be a bird, and the bird wishes to be a cloud." The atmosphere in the world is declining day by day, and people are in a state of anxiety. However, I am diligent and dedicated, striving to be innocent. For whom am I doing this integrity? Buried in my desk, constantly striving for excellence, for whom have I put in all my hard work? However, there is nothing more tragic than death of heart. As long as there is a sense of confidence, I will deal with the harsh environment to the end; Work hard without slacking off, I am searching. "Sailing alone for thousands of miles in a boat, riding the wind and waves, chasing waves and currents. After many years, I have not yet gained a new land, and I will not rest until I reach the mountain over there."

I vaguely remember that I used to be a village boy raising cattle in the countryside, a small farmer who carried the burden and worked hard. A sincere and simple temperament, as well as a hardworking spirit, are treasures that I bring from the countryside and am proud of. Of course, external factors are not allowed to interfere and destroy these qualities. Gradually, on the journey of struggle, it seems that I am gradually able to master myself.

During my university years, I served as the president of our school's Tai Chi Club. My simple information is as follows: birth, address, educational background.

Finally, sincerely, please be willing to try to get to know me and make friends with me.

Yours sincerely,

Wang Wang

The letter was sent on April 17th, 1982. Two days later, I walked out of the dormitory to have breakfast outside the school and saw Feng Qing coming from afar, dressed in sportswear. We both stopped walking at the same time.

"Hi! Good morning, do you have any classes?"

"Well, I received your letter. The writing is very good."

"Thank you! Are you free this noon? Let's eat together."

"Okay."

"At twelve o'clock, I'll meet you at the department office."

Returning to the dormitory, I borrowed an iron from my classmates to iron my pants, and then spent some time blowing my hair. At twelve o'clock, Feng Qing had changed to wearing a tight purple top and still sports pants, sitting in the library facing out. As soon as she saw me approaching the door, she automatically collected the books, picked up her backpack, and walked towards me; A few of her classmates turned to look at me.

I said lunch would be my treat, and she agreed without hesitation. Sitting in a corner of the restaurant, while eating, I carefully examined her and said, "Your parents must be very proud to have such a beautiful daughter." She remained silent, as if not surprised by these compliments.

"Is your blood type O type?"

"Um." Feng Qing smiled and said, "Everyone I know can guess that I am an O-type, it's really strange."

After a meal, the atmosphere was very good. She said she graduated from Zhongshan Women's High School, her younger sister went to Taipei First Girls' High School, her elder male cousin went to the Medical College of Taiwan University, and her father graduated from Cheng Kung University and now runs a factory.

"Opening a factory? So, your family is very wealthy! Where do you rent a house?"

"I live near Taiwan University, which is also my home. I live with my cousin and younger sister. My grandfather wants me to go back to Taoyuan every week to avoid learning bad habits in Taipei."

"Your grandfather? Oh, I haven't even seen my grandfather. He was washed away by the flood when my father was fourteen years old." I was lost in thought.

"Recently, my mother bought a new house in Taoyuan and wants to accommodate me. I plan to recruit elementary school students to teach; now I have several students."

"Now that the economy is booming and there are more children learning dance than before, teaching dance is also a good way out. By the way, how do I usually contact you?"

She immediately gave me the phone number for Taipei and said, "I will be at home at 10 pm." I put the phone number in my pocket and we walked out of the restaurant, chatting as we walked.

"Since I saw you during the speech, I have been asking about you everywhere and also asked the Director General of the The Young Women's Association. Do you know her?"

"Yes, I work with them and we are very familiar."

"She helped me investigate for a few days and told me over the phone, 'There is no such person.' I asked my schoolmates to borrow event photos from the Women's Association, but they couldn't borrow them. She said to my junior sister, 'Those who sat in the first row of that speech were all teachers; if they were students, we would all know each other.' So, when I first saw you in the dance classroom, the first thing I needed to confirm was whether you were a teacher."

"Do you think I'm a teacher?" She smiled.

"Yes! The classroom window is so narrow that when I see you dancing, I don't see anyone else dancing; while others are dancing, I can't see you."

Walking by the side of the stadium, I said, "Would the first-year students like to play around? I've been very busy. I don't know how far we are in terms of mentality?"

"I am different from ordinary college students and not very playful."

"However, I know for myself that my psychological age may be several years younger, and perhaps there won't be much difference between us."

"Well, I can tell."

We sat on the grass next to a villa, feeling cool and pleasant under the tree, about five steps apart. She clasped her hands around her chest.

"I am the only boy in my family, and I have four sisters who have all married. In addition, I have a younger sister. My mother wants me to find a girlfriend quickly. When she finds out that I'm dating a freshman, I don't know how she feels." Seeing her not speaking, I asked her, "Do everyone in your family agree with you taking the dance path?"

"My grandfather opposed it, but it was my mother who came forward to agree that I could apply for the dance department. Some of them were admitted from junior colleges, so their foundation is better than ours."

"Will there be a difference in strength?"

"Of course, there is a difference."

"Your mother loves her children very much."

"Yes, she cares about us very much. And my father sometimes scolds me."

I thought to myself, "What is there to scold for such a beautiful daughter?" Then I said, "My parents are also very kind to me, thinking that as I grow up, they will generally follow my opinions. Every Mother's Day, I express gratitude because she is so kind to me."

"I am the same, sending cards to her, but sometimes I dare not write too directly, otherwise I will blush."

"I came from a remote rural area and grew up playing. The farm is very busy, so I am good at work."

"I envy you for having a colorful childhood life, I don't have this kind of experience."

"What is your favorite subject?"

"I have been away from my desk for a long time since I went to college. I used to like biology the most, and I always got the highest marks in biology. I am also interested in Chinese studies. When I was in high school, I had a Chinese teacher who was very good to me. In addition, there is English, and now I start, I have to work harder to learn, English is very important." After a while, she asked, "Do you have any interest in music?"

"Yes, I joined the school choir in elementary school and practiced for four years. Are you interested in cooking?"

"More or less, people always have to learn! I often try saltiness, and I have to try it several times."

At this moment, the cold wind was blowing in gusts, feeling a bit uncomfortable. I said, "The days will be long in the future, and I hope to gradually increase our acquaintance. Welcome you to Nantou and see the countryside when you have time. I can also go to Taoyuan to play, right?"

"My mother is very concerned about me. She should be very good at interfering in my affairs."

"Let's talk again when we have time! Do you feel cold?"

"Well, it's a bit cold. We're going to dance ballet at three o'clock," she said as we walked. We walked into the school side by side and said goodbye to each other under the classroom building.

Chapter 4   Collision with a Wall

Overall, Feng Qing and I had a successful first date and felt extremely happy inside.

I dare not neglect her. The next day, I found time to look for her in the classroom. I asked her classmate to come into the classroom to pass messages, and all I got was a note that said:

May 3, 1982

Dear Wang Wang:

I'm very sorry, I don't think it's suitable for us to be together. My parents and friends are both against our dating, and I don't think I'm the ideal girl in your mind, so any further dating would be unnecessary. I believe you will find another good girl who truly belongs to your heart. Best wishes to you.

Sincerely,
Feng Qing

This matter cannot be forced, I can only come back disappointed. I wrote a letter to her in the evening, asking why she changed her mind so quickly. I waited for a few days, but there was no response. At night, when I make phone calls, her younger sister answers and always says, "She's not here" or "She's asleep". Once, it was a boy's voice. Her elder male cousin answered the phone and said rudely:

"Please don't bother her by calling. She just graduated from high school, what does she understand? Her family is against your relationship, and she doesn't have a good opinion of you."

Since there were boys blocking the situation, things were probably much more difficult, and my heart was mostly cooled. And in my mind, Feng Qing's smiles on me again and again come to mind. Those should all be sincere smiles

from the bottom of her heart! Can a person's decision change so quickly? A while ago, it seemed like she was interested in dating me, how could she be so hasty and turn her back on me?

Hanging up the public phone, I walked lazily into the dormitory, went to bed, and covered myself with a quilt. My roommate is a Korean international student, and when he saw my face looking ugly, he asked:

"Didn't you say that you recently met a girl from the dance department, what happened?"

"It seems to be quite difficult. The ranking of our school is far lower than that of National Taiwan University. The girl has an elder male cousin who is studying at National Taiwan University Medical School. He blocked me on the phone. It seemed that I should give up."

"What does study at National Taiwan University mean? Some friends from South Korea attend National Taiwan University, and I enter Chinese Culture University, but they are not more capable than me."

"Taiwanese people are different. The word 'Taiwan University' is enough, especially when compared to 'Chinese Culture University'."

"The person you want to socialize with is also a student of Chinese Culture University and not a student of Taiwan University. Why are you feeling inferior?"

"Currently, most young ladies consider medical school graduates as their most ideal choice. Isn't that the case with South Korea?"

"The situation is similar, but haven't you heard that most doctors are very busy, and their wives are very lonely and have many affairs? In particular, many doctors have affairs, which will also prompt their wives to have extramarital affairs in order to take revenge on her husband."

"What you're talking about is a common situation, but not all of it. The profession of a doctor is a great attraction for young ladies. Based on this alone, I think I can't compete with them."

"I have read an article that states that doctors are professions with a high loss rate, and their professional lives are also at risk among various industries, especially those who are overly busy and specialize in surgery for critically ill patients. In the field of your expertise, there is certainly the capability to surpass others, and you don't necessarily have to give up."

"Perhaps the ladies in the world don't pay much attention to what you say. Most people think that the industry that can earn a lot of money in a short period of time is the best."

I don't know exactly what Feng Qing's attitude is, I always try to make phone calls every night. Once, her younger cousin said, "She hasn't come back yet." I said, "Feng Qing once said that she would be at home after ten o'clock in the evening. Does she often delay returning home?" Her cousin seemed a bit flustered, as if she was worried that Feng Qing might be misunderstood or left a bad impression. She quickly said, "No, she won't come back very late."

But the next night, the situation changed. Her elder male cousin answered with a resolute voice, "I advise you not to call, why do you still call? Feng Qing goes out with her boyfriend every night and won't come back until after eleven o'clock."

In the face of these bad attitudes, I can tolerate them and only hope that Feng Qing will tell me in person whether to decide to socialize with others. I wrote a few letters, but she didn't reply. My letter said, "Your elder male cousin and younger cousin are very concerned about you and protect you, and I can understand them all. I sincerely admire them."

Later, her younger cousin changed her tune and said, "Feng Qing has returned, but she doesn't want to answer the phone." His elder male cousin never answered the phone again.

Chapter 5   Who said the Yellow River is vast, but a small boat can cross it

In the afternoon, I went to the classroom to find Feng Qing. The other students hadn't come yet. She was wearing a golden dress and was very beautiful. There was a book called "*Today's American Language*" on the table. I walked up to her and said hello; She didn't move at all and said slowly:

"My original intention was to be an ordinary friend with you, but I realized that your starting point was not what I imagined, so I don't want to continue dating you. I suggest you make more girlfriends."

"Where do I have the time to have multiple girlfriends? What is my starting point? No problem, right? I said that I hope to have a long-term relationship and slowly get to know each other. One day, if you think I can date you, then continue to date me; if you feel it is not suitable for you, you can ask me to leave. I know that relationships do not need to be forced."

The girls walked into the classroom in groups of two or three, and Feng Qing got up to talk to her classmates, doing some chores with each other. After a while, a girl walked up to me and said, "May I go outside and have a few words with you?"

"Okay," I followed her out of the classroom.

The unfamiliar girl said, "Feng Qing already has a boyfriend. She met you and originally just wanted to be an ordinary friend, but you were too serious. She felt scared. She knows you are a good boy and have never encountered setbacks. She is unwilling to hurt you, and this letter is for you."

I took the letter over, feeling a bit lost in my soul and unsure what to do. "Could you please ask her to come out for a conversation? If she decides that I won't come again, I won't come again. I just want to hear her explain in person."

She went in to invite Feng Qing and quickly came out to answer, "Feng Qing doesn't want to come out."

"What does she mean? Does she want me to never come again?"

"No, it's not."

I left the classroom in a daze, opening the letter as I walked. The letter reads:

May 10th, 1982

Dear Wang Wang:

I'm sorry, I already have a boyfriend. He is currently a third-year student at National Taiwan University Medical School, and I get along very well with him.

You misunderstood my original intention from the beginning, I just wanted to be an ordinary friend with you......

......Who said the Yellow River is vast, but a small boat can cross it."

Sincerely,
Feng Qing

She said at the beginning of the letter that she already had a boyfriend. I was greatly disappointed and tore up the letter on the spot, threw it into the trash can, and quickly walked back to the dormitory. At the entrance of the dormitory, I happened to meet my student elder sister from the literary institute. She said:

"I heard that your behavior has been a bit excessive recently, which scared a freshman girl."

"Is that right? I don't think it's my fault! She didn't even answer the phone, no wonder small things turned into big things; I'm not that scary person. Just now I received a reply from her saying she already has a boyfriend from National Taiwan University. I tore up the letter and it's over."

"Think of it as a valuable experience."

"I was just hit too hard and didn't finish reading the letter before I tore it up. I don't know what she wrote, as if the last sentence was: "Who said the Yellow River is vast, but a small boat can cross it.""

"Really? If she writes that way, does it imply that you still have hope to pursue?"

"Oh dear! Isn't that so? It depends on what's written before and after! How could I be so confused! But why did she write such hurtful words at the beginning of the letter?" I said anxiously, "I'm going to get the letter back and look at it carefully."

Unfortunately, after running back, I found that all the contents of the trash can had been taken away by the cleaning staff.

Chapter 6　Brings Her Beautiful Memories

Is Feng Qing's letter carrying a mystery? With the disappearance of the letter, it is no longer verifiable; These speculations once again plunged me into confusion.

When I entered the literary research institute, Professor Wang also came to care about me, and he said:

"Telephone communication is not as good as face-to-face communication. Telephone communication is a cold thing. Writing some letters is also good. A girl starts making friends with the opposite sex until she gets married in the future. If a man is considerate enough, writing some letters can keep her for life and leave beautiful memories. Isn't that great?"

I agree with Professor Wang's view, so I walked into the bookstore to buy some cards and wrote:

Dear Feng Qing:

"Even if there are flowers and moons, how can one endure the absence of wine and the other person?" It is said that the scenery of mountains and rivers, spring flowers and autumn moons are enough to make one feel relaxed and intoxicated. I have tried to appreciate, but I always feel that there is something missing, but I can't say it; Sometimes I even feel dull or depressed. Do you know? Perfect as you, mountains and rivers can be abandoned. If we can share the scenery and appreciate life together, we will definitely be able to enjoy extreme happiness together. This is for Feng Qing, who made me infatuated at first sight.

Unable to erase all infatuation, unable to speak. Every time I want to meet you, my heart is filled with joy and fear; And you always have a cold attitude, "It's so difficult to deal with!" Have you ever known that you have brought me great pain? Please pity me, there is only one you in my mind, Feng Qing.

Ancient gentlemen always worried about their own decay along with flowers, plants, and trees. I consciously wanted to work hard and not only become a righteous gentleman, but also create achievements and emulate ancient celebrities. I know this is a very difficult task, but you have shown me the dawn. If I could hold onto you, I would confidently grasp the entire life and create a bright future to present to you, Feng Qing.

I don't ask for quick friendship, I just hope you give me a smile and talk to me. This is when you start trying to get to know me. Do you think so? Feng Qing.

Yours sincerely,

Wang Wang

After sending out the card, I called Feng Qing in the evening, but her younger sister refused to answer and only gently placed the receiver on the table. I can hear the voice of the other person's conversation and movements. A few minutes later, the phone was disconnected.

Chapter 7   Economic Topics

In the research room, I envy others who are in the mood to read, but I always feel uneasy. A senior student inquired:

"What's happening with making girlfriend now? Is there any progress?"

"No, she avoided meeting up and claimed to have a boyfriend who was in his third year at National Taiwan University. I tried to verify this matter. Ah! comparing Taiwan University with Cultural University is really nerve-racking!"

"Not necessarily," Teacher Wang stopped flipping through his books and turned his head, saying,"The admission rate for the joint college entrance examination is only 25%. Those who can get into college are all excellent. I used to be the secretary of the institute, and a student who graduated from National Taiwan University came to take our graduate school entrance examination. As a result, he was only on the waiting list and was not admitted later. National Taiwan University is not necessarily that good."

"That's it! And you're a graduate student, your opponent is only a college student." The senior encouraged me with these words and asked, "What does her family do?"

"She said her family runs a factory, and I think she's quite wealthy. Her family and relatives all receive higher education, no wonder the standards are set high."

"Most modern women do not have the spirit of traditional women's 'hard work'. When dating, in addition to love, most of them carefully consider the issue of bread. In such a highly material civilization society, love without bread can be particularly sad."

"I think so too." I accepted Teacher Wang's guidance and was momentarily disinterested to talk more. At this moment, I remembered a month ago when my mother came to Taipei and learned that I was currently interested in having a girlfriend, but there was no progress yet. She said, "Our family has over seven hectares of land. Let the other party know, and she should be very reassured." I said bluntly to my mother at that time, "I don't want to bring up the topic of money and property to make friends, so as not to confuse my judgment of a person." My mother has always believed that female morality is important, so she stopped talking too much. Now, Teacher Wang's words seem to be a real-life issue that I have overlooked. Perhaps I should do some self reflection and self adjustment.

My thoughts are a bit confused, thinking: "When Feng Qing was on the date, she heard that I was a child from the countryside and I didn't mention anything about wealth. She looked envious and gave me a phone number. Her personality was admirable. I said something about the countryside. Would her family mistakenly think that my family is in a poor situation? If she had such economic doubts, of course she would hesitate. Oh, is it because they have doubts about my family situation that I have encountered various difficulties recently?"

Recently, Feng Qing has rejected my letter and has been keeping it in the mailbox of the dance department. I had to overcome it this time. I rushed back to my dormitory and wrote another letter, asking my roommate from South Korea to personally deliver the letter to Feng Qing's class. The letter told her about my family's financial situation.

The next morning, the letter was delivered successfully. In the afternoon, during class time, I ran to the back door of the classroom to see Feng Qing's reaction after reading the letter. She was found sitting in the last row, with everyone sitting upright listening, except for her frowning and sleeping on the table; I looked at her from a very close distance.

There are not many times when I can visit her. It has to be when I don't have classes and she happens to have classes. Therefore, she can predict which class I might go to see her. After a few days, I couldn't wait for a reply. During class time, I went to visit again. On this day, she was dressed in gorgeous attire and a long skirt, which was the most exquisite attire she had ever worn since we met. At first glance, I was mesmerized by it for a long time, bewildered and unaware. I thought to myself, "She is wearing such beautiful clothes, how disappointing it would be if there were a conflict between me and her!" Finally, I had to leave the classroom and write to tell her that I had visited her in the classroom, asking her to agree to socialize with me.

The Literature Research Institute is on the third floor, and the Dance Department is on the first floor, very close. My senior sister started a Chinese language class in the dance department, so it was easy to hear about it. When I entered the research room, there were a lot of rumors and noise, and the voices of criticism or affirmation from senior students in the research institute flooded in.

"If you don't rush at first and don't scare her, you should succeed. Feng Qing doesn't have any obstacles or a boyfriend from Taiwan University."

"Feng Qing's classmates said, 'Feng Qing showed them the letters and cards you wrote, and they all said that the content you wrote was too……'that'!'"

"They said, 'He is very good at writing and has a good personality.'"

Some of these words undoubtedly added a lot of confidence to me, and of course, I am willing to patiently wait. The next day, the seniors received new rumors and said to me:

"Take your time, you should have succeeded. I heard you were begging for speed; you were too anxious and even messed up the situation. How can you ask if someone can cook when you first meet her?"

"No, that's not what I said. I just asked her if she has any interest in cooking."

Another student sister walked over and said, "When you first met her, you told the dance department student that your mother wanted you to get married quickly, is this true? Our guess is completely correct. You have said all the things that shouldn't be said. She is actually not pursued by anyone, there are no obstacles, and these are all guessed by us."

I thought to myself, "Why are there so many rumors and so many people who seem to be stirring up the news? Am I really doing so much wrong?" At that time, my mood was really low and I was almost angry. Feeling discouraged, I walked to the school's mail room and found that the letter I had written to Feng Qing the other day was still in their mailbox and had not been taken away. So, I took it out and put it in my pocket; I plan to go directly to the classroom and hand it to her.

After the seventh class, I stood outside the classroom and exchanged a distant glance with Feng Qing in the classroom. At the beginning of the eighth class, I was reading newspapers on the newspaper rack in the nearby corridor; Soon, I walked back to the classroom and waited. Finally, class was over, and Feng Qing quickly rushed out of the front door alone, running downstairs. I quickly chased after her; Running to the stairs on the fifth floor, she stopped and said shyly and coquettishly:

"I don't want to see you."

I was about to speak when she started running upstairs again, shouting her classmate's name, 'Ellen, Ellen'. The two of them arrived at the elevator, and she approached her classmate and spoke in a low voice. There were over a dozen people waiting for the elevator in front of me, and I was pacing along with my back to her. They all turned around to look at me.

The elevator door had opened, I followed in quickly. After going downstairs, Feng Qing walked side by side with a classmate, and I just followed. After a while, the three of us stopped walking at the same time.

"The letter I gave you, you haven't taken it yet, it's in the mailbox."

"She doesn't want to take it, so don't force her."

"No, no one helped her with it."

Feng Qing accepted my letter and I just watched her leave.

Chapter 8   Destruction

When I returned to my hometown, my mother was a bit unfamiliar with girls majoring in dance. She said: "Last time I went to Taipei, I asked you to bring her to show me. You said it wasn't time yet, so what's happening now? Is a young lady who loves dancing suitable for our rural child to socialize with? We rural people are frugal and hardworking. What if she only wants to play and can't endure hardship? We are so busy working in the fields, and the situation of our family may not be appreciated by urban people, so we must pay attention to this. Are girls from other departments more suitable for us? Moreover, we cannot just be obsessed with someone's beautiful appearance, as female morality is very important."

"Mom, it's not that beautiful girls have bad morals."

My mother has been the "eldest sister" of the family since childhood, and even her own siblings are genuinely afraid because she is serious and doesn't joke casually. In my heart, she is a hardworking, rational, and dignified mother with a kind heart.

"You said she was making things difficult for you, could she be a very proud girl?"

"It's not like that! It's just that the young lady was just starting to find it so fun! Those situations are normal, I'll keep my eyes wide open."

Farewell to my hometown, I plan to spend the night at my third sister's house in Yonghe. My third sister asked me about Feng Qing, and I said, "It hasn't been successful yet, but I find it very interesting. She lives in Gongguan, very close to here. We live on one end of the bridge, and she lives on the other end."

My brother-in-law said, "Make a phone call and ask if she wants to come."

"She can't come now; at most I'll try to greet her on the phone."

I stood next to my brother-in-law and dialed the phone, just to say hello to Feng Qing. But her younger cousin picked up the phone and said, "She's out. She's out on a date with her boyfriend." With a 'card' sound, she hung up the phone. I was stunned for a long time, not knowing how to put down the receiver.

Afterwards, my four elder sisters and one younger sister often discussed my affairs over the phone because they felt like I was being manipulated and wondered if it was all just my wishful thinking? Some are worried that I will

neglect my studies, ruin my grades, and possibly ruin my bright future. Some people calculated the number of strokes in her name, saying that her fate is a "dilemma", and then tell our mother that they only have one younger brother, so they must consider everything for him. Finally, someone proposed opposing my association with Feng Qing; My family and I inevitably have conflicting opinions at this time.

I believe my sisters are all good for me, and if Feng Qing doesn't come forward quickly to clarify some doubts, this friendship is about to face crisis. On May 29th, I sent a letter to Feng Qing:

May.29.1982

Feng Qing:

I heard that in fact, you don't have a really good boyfriend from Taiwan University, is that true? I am delighted to hear such news.

April 12th, the first time I saw you, was an unforgettable and important day. Up to now, over forty nights of tossing and turning, with no sleep at all, have become extremely restless. My dress belt is gradually widening, my figure is haggard, my family and friends show more pity for me. Can you bear to continue this way of handling it?

Choosing someone based on beauty alone, once their beauty fades, the love will fade. It's not like that when two people pay attention to the spiritual understanding; it's just that the longer they go by, the more they understand how to cherish each other. Last time I went home, I listened to my loving mother's instructions, telling me not to neglect women's virtues. I only regret that you have been avoiding conversation. On May 31st, I will meet you at the department office.

Sincerely,
Wang Wang

Two days later, I went to the dance department office to find Feng Qing. She sat in the office reading a book and noticed that I was coming. She spoke to her classmates and then walked towards me together, facing each other at the door.

"Are you in the same class?"

"Yes, we are all in the same class."

"Talking about personal matters, why are there so many people?"

A girl in front couldn't resist my accusing gaze and walked into the room with a bit of embarrassment.

"I have already told you not to come to me; And you come to me again. I tell you, I don't like being friends with you."

"Feng Qing's boyfriend originally planned to go up the mountain together today."

"Can we have lunch together at noon?" I asked her with a very gentle attitude.

"No, I'm not happy with you," she said and turned in with a few girls.

At this time, I deeply regretted that the previous letter had ruined the good thing, and I had to leave with heavy steps. Go back to the dormitory and write a letter of apology.

Dear Feng Qing:

Who would have expected a girl's heart to be so sensitive? Of course, I made a mistake, but it was really unintentional.

If it weren't for the pursuit of such a beautiful woman, why did I search from the past to today? Since I am always looking forward to establishing this

friendship, why should I deliberately provoke you? If I have the slightest distrust of your character, how can I be willing to pursue it without giving up?

The previous letter was not malicious. I not only appreciate your extraordinary appearance, but also am willing to pursue spiritual harmony and even eternal concern.

My mother is the kindest elder, who cares for me day and night. Of course, I also think about her physical and mental health. A few days ago, when I described you as outstanding and extraordinary, she felt happy. As for telling me to "pay attention to female virtues", this is probably the case for loving mothers all over the world.

Let me tell you from the bottom of my heart that I firmly believe that you are a good girl with both appearance and virtue, yet I am so difficult to speak up.

If we are destined, let's meet during the summer vacation! As courtesy, I look forward to hearing from you and giving me your Taoyuan mailing address.

Sincerely,
Wang Wang

After three days, the apology letter was still left in the mailbox and she didn't take it away. In the evening, a student sister hurriedly walked into the literary institute and said with a serious expression, "I heard you've been bothering her, she's in pain and wants to take a break from school." The students and seniors present were in a great uproar, with only criticism and ridicule in one sentence and another. My emotions got a bit out of control and I said, "You're like blind people feeling an elephant, you don't know the whole situation!"

Professor Wang then walked in with a worried expression and whispered, "Do you know that?"

"I see." I said weakly, "Everyone takes this matter seriously, that's what I feel the most helpless about. In fact, my pace is already very slow."

"Have there been any disputes?"

"My family has a slight prejudice against the girl majoring in dance. I wrote her a letter and told her frankly, but I can trust her. Also, a while ago, many people said she didn't actually have a boyfriend from Taiwan University. I was happy, but I accidentally pointed this out in the letter."

"Dancing is a great art, what's wrong with it? Also, regarding the boyfriend at National Taiwan University, you should take it as a real thing and not disclose it."

The people present felt that things were not easy to tidy up, so they went to their own business.

At night, her younger sister received my phone call with a very aggressive attitude and immediately hung up. I called again and she said, "If you have anything, speak up quickly."

"Actually, I didn't mean to harm Feng Qing."

"I tell you; she already has a boyfriend and is very close. If you have anything to do, you can directly come to her to solve it. You often call, and you don't listen to advice. I'm about to take an exam, do you know?"

"The pursuit of a beautiful girl is the wish of every man. Please don't stop me, okay?" I thought she was willing to listen. After a while, I said, "I'm very sorry to disturb your peace, but I didn't mean to disturb you. If Feng Qing answered the phone well, how could I disturb you? I really did something wrong and said something I shouldn't have said, which made her sad, so I want to apologize to her. Can you please persuade her to come get the letter?"

"I can help you persuade her, but whether she is willing to take it or not is her business, I don't care." Her tone seemed to ease a lot.

I walked to the mailbox, retrieved the letter I wrote on May 31st, opened it, and added a note:

Dear Feng Qing:

I didn't mean to hurt you, but I was misunderstood by you. I suffer more than you can imagine.

I actually heard that you plan to apply for a suspension of study. Sure enough, by then, you will receive a message - I will also suspend my studies. Because going to school no longer means anything to me. Could you please forgive my mistake?

Sincerely,
Wang Wang

This time, Feng Qing received the letter. And gave a reply letter:

Wang Wang:

Emotional matters cannot be forced. You know it well, but why bother to force each other. I believe that seeing each other again can only increase our unnecessary troubles. I believe you also don't want to see me worry about this. Please put yourself in my shoes and think about it! We have no chance. Wishing you a bright future, this is also my last reply.

Sincerely,
Feng Qing

I was just frustrated when I saw that she had circled the words "put yourself in my shoes" and I didn't know what to do with it. In the blink of an eye, summer vacation is approaching, and without obtaining an address, there is no way to contact. In the evening, I still bravely called, but her elder male cousin appeared again, consistently insulting me with cold words, which I couldn't handle. Just say, "I have received her reply. Could you please convey that I will be looking for her at the exam room tomorrow?"

After the exam, Feng Qing walked out of the examination room. On this day, she was wearing fashionable and trendy clothing, with the length of her pants only reaching her calves, and her hair specially combed. Originally a beautiful girl, coupled with deliberate attire, the dazzling and eye-catching look really makes everyone around her look pale.

I approached to talk to her, but she turned away and ignored me; I followed closely, and she smiled slightly, unwilling to stop.

"Listen to me! Can you stop?" I advanced and reached out to stop her. She turned around and walked back. I am once again ahead, trying to stop her. She finally stopped, looked down at the ground, and said softly and gently, "I don't want to listen." After that, she walked back.

Unexpectedly, her classmates saw injustice on the way, and someone blocked my way and surrounded me one after another.

"See? She ignored you. There's still an exam today, how can you come and harass?"

"It's not harassment, I just want to see her. If I don't come today, the summer vacation is coming soon. How can I find her?"

"She told you that she already has a boyfriend. You almost made her drop out of school, so what are you doing here? You are clearly damaging your own character."

"You are good to her, I know. However, this is a private matter between her and me. Why are there so many people in charge? If you want to drive me away, only she is qualified. Please don't intervene."

"You're too disrespectful!" Someone added.

"Feng Qing, come and ask him to leave, don't let him tangle up here."

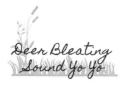

Feng Qing only stood far away, with his back to me, as if she had no intention of getting involved in this dispute. These 'evil girls' indeed had powerful lip guns and tongue swords, and I was angrily driven away amidst their explosive sounds.

Chapter 9   Please Choose

The summer vacation has already begun, and I asked my younger brother and sister from the Chinese department to help me inquire about Feng Qing's Taoyuan phone number and address. Within a few days, I did find out. I don't know if these messages are correct, so I tried to call Feng Qing at Gongguan, and it happened that her classmates picked it up, and it seemed that several classmates were present. I said:

"It's summer vacation. I don't know if Feng Qing will go back to Taoyuan to live. Is her home on Chenggong Road in Taoyuan City? Is the phone number......"

Her classmate laughed while repeating, "Is her home on Chenggong Road in Taoyuan City......" Through the phone, I heard a burst of laughter from the other party. After laughing for a while, the student picked up the receiver again and said, "I'm sorry, Feng Qing said she won't answer." Then she hung up the phone.

Although Feng Qing doesn't answer, I intuitively believe that these Taoyuan addresses and phone numbers should be correct. And the other party's scene seemed relaxed and pleasant, it's hard to imagine the group of people who cursed each other with me on the day of the final exam now being able to have a friendly conversation with me.

I am obviously much haggard, and many seniors continue to care about me, while I can only complain:

"She doesn't handle things on her own and would rather entrust her own affairs to cousins, or classmates in class, which I don't agree with. If someone has bad intentions and does some provocative behavior in the middle, will she have enough ability to deal with it? This situation makes me uneasy."

"You encourage her to come forward! For example, throwing out some questions that make her think of 'what to do', and then she will find a way to solve it. You can't just be busy on your side, but she's happy and leisurely."

I thought for a while and planned to write a letter, along with a few photos, to Taoyuan to see how she would handle it.

Dear Feng Qing:

A great mother warned her son, "Be polite to any woman! That doesn't mean they are noble, but it represents your demeanor." If you belittle me, I think this is an unexpected absurdity.

I saw a pair of sapphire double lion seals in a department store, priced at a thousand yuan. I bought it with great satisfaction and admired its exquisiteness and preciousness. Imagine if it were brought to the door by a vendor to sell, I might hesitate for a while and give up. Today, I don't know how to prove to you that I have the enthusiasm of a hawker and the quality of a pair of sapphires in a department store.

At the beginning, you and I happily made a promise - a mundane relationship, a long-term experience, I believe you have not forgotten. Now, I am exhausted, haggard in appearance, and heartbroken in heart. What are your intentions?

When eating, there is a kind of person who likes to rummage on the plate and finally pick out the food he likes; there is another kind of person who looks with his eyes and then reaches out to take it; I would like to be the latter. I have observed carefully, there are many friends, and I have always confirmed that you are beautiful and extraordinary.

How many troubles and confusions have been completely rejected by me; How many people mock me for giving up near and seeking far, and I can ignore it; All persistence is for you. Please carefully observe this sincere and unchanging heart and give me an answer.

PS. Attached are six photos

Sincerely,

Wang Wang

I waited for a week, but there was no response. I called Gongguan and her younger cousin answered, saying, "Feng Qing and her younger sister went to the United States yesterday."

"May I ask if she has received a letter at home."

"Received, Feng Qing's mother has also seen the photos. Feng Qing advised you many times, but you didn't listen; she hopes you don't waste your time anymore. Feng Qing's mother advised her to have a good conversation with you and ask you not to waste your time on her anymore."

"I......" I couldn't answer for a moment. "I may be too stubborn,...... Could you please convey that just send my photos back? I don't want to talk to her."

"Okay, I'll ask Feng Qing's mother to send it to you. I'm in my third year of high school and I'm busy with homework. Please don't call me again." Her attitude was always gentle and polite.

"Okay."

At this time, the school's publishing department recruited dozens of students to start working on dictionary revision, most of them were students from the Chinese Department. I was in graduate school, and in the work group, I was a foreman. My younger siblings have heard a lot about Feng Qing and me, and some are curious. And I am currently in a stage of "losing face", so I try to keep a low profile and handle most questions with caution, such as smiling without answering.

After waiting for a week, I didn't receive the photo returned by Feng Qing's mother. The more I thought about it, the more I became puzzled. I thought to myself, "No matter what the outcome, maybe it would be better to meet and talk about it once." So, I tried to make a call to Taoyuan, and it was answered by a child. I asked:

"May I ask if Feng Qing has returned?"

"She went to study English and hasn't come back yet."

I finally realized that she didn't really go to the United States, but I could only pretend not to know. In the evening, I called again, and her father answered the phone, saying:

"She's not here, she's gone to the United States."

"I am a student at Chinese Culture University. Since she has not yet returned to Taiwan, I will contact her again after she returns."

"……" The other party remained silent.

"Goodbye," I politely hung up.

Upon learning that I had made a promise, Feng Qing immediately requested her mother to return the photos and attached a letter, stating:

Dear Wang:

A few days ago, I received a letter and photos sent to my daughter. As she was away, I replied on her behalf.

I learned from the letter that Wang is a promising young man with excellent conditions. You should broaden your horizons, because my daughter had a great hometown boyfriend when she was in high school, and he is currently studying at National Taiwan University. So as parents, we don't want her to have too many emotional troubles. We hope you can understand. It's easy to find a satisfactory girl on your terms.

Along with sending this letter, I will also return your photos to you. I hope you understand and do not call or write again.

Sincerely,

Aunt Feng

The persuasion of this letter is invalid. According to my personal guess, it was after I promised to find her again that Feng Qing decided to ask her mother to write this. Moreover, it was unheard of for her to start dating boyfriend early in high school. After twenty days, I called Gongguan and Feng Qing's elder male cousin answered the phone, saying:

"Feng Qing has not returned to Taiwan yet," he said with an unfriendly attitude. "Feng Qing's mother has already told you, why are you still calling?"

"……" I didn't answer, just stuck to the receiver.

"Feng Qing ignored you. You're just wishful thinking, don't you know?"

"I heard that Feng Qing's mother wants her to have a conversation with me, so I think it's better to have a conversation," I said in a gentle tone.

"Oh!……" He seemed like a deflated balloon, suddenly unable to speak, "……that's the case!…… Alright, you can make an agreement again in the future."

I stayed at home for two days, and when I returned to school again, I had a backpack on my shoulders and a handbag in my hand. I met Feng Qing on the campus road, and we both stopped walking at the same time.

"I returned home the day before yesterday," she looked down at the ground.

"Do you want to talk? Are you busy?"

She said gently, "I'm registering for the dance camp." Later, she said, "I don't think there's much to talk about." After that, she left on her own and left me there.

I froze for a few seconds before feeling too heavy a burden on my shoulders and hands. So, I rushed back to the dormitory, unloaded my backpack, washed my face, and ran out again, standing on the balcony upstairs and looking down. On the square downstairs, there were some tables and chairs set up, and young friends went to register one after another. Feng Qing and her classmates were busy accepting the application, and her face lit up with a smile. Her happy expression at this moment was the kind I wanted to see the most. It was precisely to preserve her happy state that I didn't want to go hastily today to avoid damaging the scenery.

In the evening, I called Gongguan and Feng Qing's younger cousin answered, saying:

"Didn't Feng Qing go abroad?"

"No, she has returned home. This afternoon, we met on campus and she said she came back the day before yesterday."

"Oh......" She was chuckling.

"Could you please persuade her to have a frank conversation with me?"

"I'll give it a try."

When working in the publishing department, I didn't like to talk about Feng Qing with my younger classmates, but there were always a few who took the initiative to show concern. Some students even know that my heart already belongs to someone else, but when they have time, they still like to joke with me. Some ask me to help her interpret the relationship between the lines on her hands and their destiny, some offer famous poems to appreciate, and some girls always ask, "When will you treat me to ice?" or want to find a chance to have dinner together. My principle is to show them a clear attitude and let them know that my heart is on the dance department side, because I don't want to delay the good opportunity for others to find another partner. At the same time, emotions don't need to be explained too much. If someone secretly falls in love with me, I firmly believe in that sentence: Emotions are temporary, time can naturally solve problems, and there's no need to worry or be busy explaining anything now. Therefore, "pretending not to know" is my usual method.

I waited and waited, but couldn't wait for Feng Qing's reply, so I had to call again. His elder male cousin received it and said:

"I want to advise you to know the difficulties and automatically exit because your hope is slim."

"……" My anger rose and I didn't say a word.

"Feng Qing's boyfriend is my classmate, they are already very close and don't want anyone else to intervene."

"Can you arrange time for me to talk on the phone?"

"What's up? "

"If it's okay, just say goodbye."

"Okay, you'll call at eleven o'clock."

At eleven o'clock, I called and Feng Qing immediately answered. I said very gently, "Feng Qing, why do you always avoid talking?"

"Wang Wang, I really have a boyfriend now. Please don't call again."

"Alright, bless you."

Returning to the dormitory, I expressed deep sorrow and dissatisfaction with her elder male cousin's manipulation of the overall situation, thinking to myself, "Unless Feng Qing personally rejects me, I will never be willing to accept it."

So, I took up my pen again and wrote a letter:

Dear Feng Qing:

As summer sets, in the Campanian plain on the outskirts of Rome......

The fields and hills shrouded in the dark dusk were so silent, without a sound. The sheep were mostly leisurely grazing and slowly walking towards the sheep prison - this is the ruins of the capital city of the Roman Empire. Isn't there a magnificent king here in ancient times who reigned over the three armies, wielding the power of life, death, and seizure, and arrogating himself to the world? Nowadays, there is not even a tree to praise, only hazelnut trees are everywhere.

Where is the towering dome of the marble palace of Emperor Augustus now located? I only saw a whole expanse of barren grass, leaving behind only relics that wanderers from other lands came to mourn.

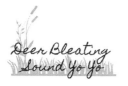
But there is still a small tower left over there, hidden in the tower is a girl with blonde hair and white face, swallowing her breath and looking around for her lover in the nightclub? As soon as the lover arrived, they suddenly caught up and hugged each other silently.

The chariots of gold, the army of millions, are now in ruins, with no shadow left; However, the love between men and women has its unchanging eternity; Even after thousands of years, it cannot be eliminated. The troubles of centuries, their victories, glory, and gold, have all disappeared, and only love is supreme.

The above is the general idea of "*Love among the Ruins*" written by the great British poet Robert Browning in the Victorian era. Let us take a look at the immortal poems praising love such as the sonnets written by Mrs. Browning. How intoxicating it is! Their love lasted forever and they were a very famous couple in the history of British literature. Kukawa Hakumura said: "The eternal capital" is not Rome, but love.

A Western scholar once said, 'No husband dares to fully reveal his true emotional life while his wife is still alive.' This argument is widely accepted. But the fact is not entirely as he said, for example, in Krosky's book *"The Gospel of Love"*, he clearly puts forward the opposite view, saying: "If you believe that he will not betray you, he will naturally not betray you. Because if he betrays you, he not only betrays you, but also betrays your sincere belief, which is enough to make him even more unwilling to betray you. So, you can really take the risk of believing, you have a confidence, and you will increase the security of your love." I strongly agree with this statement.

Your elder male cousin cursed me fiercely, indicating that you have a strong aversion to me. I don't know why. In fact, love has no distinction between classes.

If you had written to dissuade me a few days ago, I wouldn't have troubled you anymore; But you evaded and didn't reply, which made me feel so embarrassed.

Why can I withstand one and another blow? Because I am certain of your simplicity and innocence. I remember the first time we had a meeting, you gave me your phone number without considering it. You welcomed me to find you and promised to visit the central region. This is truly Feng Qing, who has not lost your self determination. Unexpectedly, there was a time when others made you indecisive; Adding my undeserved card caused you to hesitate.

I hope you can carefully recognize this most dedicated and precious relationship. I have strict self-discipline in dealing with people and things, and I cannot say everything in just a few words. If you refuse me, I feel sorry for you. Promise me to have gentle and polite communication and interaction between us, okay? If you really want to refuse me, I only request a gentle and sincere refusal letter.

Yours sincerely,

Wang Wang

On the morning of July 28th, carrying the letter, I met Feng Qing in the hallway outside the dance department office. I stepped forward to block the way, and she only lowered her head and whispered:

"Please......"

"This letter is for you."

Feng Qing didn't say a word, received the letter, and entered the office.

In early autumn, it is cool on the evening, and the wind and moon are very beautiful. But for me, who is suffering, it doesn't mean much. Even if this letter was handed to Feng Qing in person, after a long period of time, she still did not respond at all. I called again, just asking for trouble, but She didn't answer.

Chapter 10   Conflict

Feng Qing procrastinated intentionally or unintentionally, and finally the summer vacation was over. In the evening, I called to Gongguan. Her younger sister answered:

"She's not here. why is your last time endless?"

Her words were really difficult to answer. From her perspective, accusing me of not keeping my word is somewhat true, but I can't escape it! Feng Qing always responds to me; how could I not understand? But this is a situation that others are not aware of. I was filled with grievances and could only endure it. I replied, "Because I haven't had a chance to talk to her." After a while, I said, "May I ask if she will come back tonight?"

"Not necessarily."

"I am currently under the bus stop sign on Route 253 at Gongguan. Could you please convey it and ask her to come out to meet? If she doesn't come out, I will wait until dawn."

"Okay."

I sat on the iron chair on the sidewalk and made a decision calmly: "As long as she comes out and makes it clear, I will accept it happily. I don't want to be ridiculed by some people anymore, and I don't want to cause any problems."

By twelve o'clock, there were no buses and the shops were turning off their lights one by one. It's impossible for her to come so late, but I just want to keep my word. Sit still. Half an hour later, four police officers rode motorcycles and slowly patrolled the road. I stood there, ignoring them. They stopped and looked at me carefully; After a few seconds, without speaking, they continued to ride forward.

Then, there was a vacuum cleaner truck in the middle of the road, slowly moving forward. Another water truck passed quickly and suddenly sprayed water along the roadside. I couldn't avoid it and my pants were mostly wet.

Time is getting late; the weather is turning cooler. I have a newspaper lining my belly and back inside my clothes, leaving a newspaper wrapped around my wet pants. The mosquito bombardment came almost without interruption, and I had to be busy waving them.

Late at night, taxis were running at double speed. Many empty taxis stopped in front of me and looked around for a second or two, but I ignored them. So, I lay on the back of the chair pretending to sleep, so as not to cause such trouble for the taxi.

Until the sky turned gray, I aimed in the direction of Taipei Station and slowly strolled over. There were a few figures on the roadside, all of them were cleaning crews busy cleaning out trash cans. Arrive at Taipei Station and board the morning bus 301. Unexpectedly, this bus was actually full of passengers, all of whom were wearing sportswear and going up Yangmingshan.

As soon as I got into the bus, I immediately fell asleep. I felt the bus shake suddenly and arrived at the school. Enter the dormitory, my goodness! In the mirror, I turned into a small pockmarked face, covered in red spots bitten by mosquitoes.

In the blink of an eye, after half a semester, perhaps Feng Qing thought she was only a sophomore and everything could be handled slowly.

One afternoon, I met them at the bus waiting area and glanced at each other from afar. They went nearby to buy bread, and then Feng Qing walked up to me alone and said:

"You need to write paper, time is precious. Don't follow me down the mountain, okay?"

"Don't tell me, I'll go down the mountain," I replied in a low voice.

After a moment of confrontation, Feng Qing walked up to her classmates and had a few words. One of them approached me and said:

"Could you please not come down the mountain with us? What do you have to say? Let's go talk in the classroom!"

"I have something to talk to her about. There are too many people here, so we must go to the foot of the mountain. Please tell her that I will definitely not follow her to Gongguan. Please rest assured."

Her classmate walked back to Feng Qing and conveyed my intention.

When we got on the bus, it was very crowded. Feng Qing sat on the stainless steel bar in front. The three girls took turns eating a loaf of bread, each taking a big bite. I stood behind them and watched.

They got off the bus together in Shilin, and I got off the bus too. Walking to the roadside snack stand, they sat around; I stood in the distance, and after a while, I walked over in three or two steps and sat down opposite. Say:

"Could you please give me a chance to talk to Feng Qing alone?"

"Not good," Feng Qing answered first.

"Did you hear that?" Her classmate said with a domineering attitude, "She said 'not good'. She has already made it clear to you that she……"

"That's enough." I stopped her loudly and said," I think there are too few people who would sincerely help their friends. What are your intentions? To frame her? Or help her? You need to review and self-reflect."

"Why do you say such things? You……"

"I'm angry," I shouted over her with a loud voice, "I'm just speaking frankly." Then I stood up and said, "Alright, Feng Qing, let's cut it all at once, I'm serious."

I quickly walked away; Feng Qing didn't say a word.

I returned to the mountain and specifically wrote a letter:

November 7th, 1982

Feng Qing:

A girl said, "I really like boys writing letters, even if I don't like them. This is a common trait among girls, so I can affirm myself." "He often says, 'If you don't want to socialize, tell me straight away.' But after I finish reading it, I put it aside and just ignore it." After listening to this, I am extremely sad.

You are kind enough because you have been stopping me and reminding me. Thank you very much.

People need to have confidence, but being too confident makes me fail. In fact, apart from being overly straightforward, I don't think I made too much mistakes. Moreover, being straightforward has its own loveliness, and I firmly believe that confidants will appreciate it.

You often get angry with me, and I really hope it's a momentary anger, not a fundamental 'dislike'. I can't be sure what the answer is.

The smile you once gave me, which has captivated me to this day, is too tragic. There are many people with better knowledge and cultivation than me. I believe that with your shrewd vision, you will be able to make the most correct choice. Best wishes to you. I miss you very much now, but I will forget these things day by day; At appropriate times, also try to get to know other girls.

Sincerely,
Wang Wang

Chapter 11   Moving to accommodation on the mountain

On November 17th, I returned from the foot of the mountain and got off at the "Shanzai Hou" station. As I was about to enter the campus on foot, I happened to see Feng Qing walking side by side with a girl. Curiosity drove me to pay attention to her whereabouts, as we were about a few tens of meters apart. Suddenly, they turned a corner and entered an American style bungalow painted in red and white. I thought they were coming to visit friends, but perhaps they would come out soon. Therefore, I hesitated for a long time and couldn't bear to leave.

Strangely, after more than an hour, they still couldn't come out. So, I tried to call Gongguan, and her younger cousin answered the phone and said:

"Feng Qing is not here. May I ask who you are?"

"I'm Wang Wang." After a pause, I said again," Recently, I'm getting sick."

"I can't help it, I'm sorry…… I'm very sorry." She hung up politely.

After waiting for another half hour, I called Gongguan again and her younger cousin answered the phone again.

"Hello, this is Wang Wang."

"Feng Qing has already moved up the mountain and will not return here."

"She lives on the mountain?" I was surprised. "So, I've already seen where she lives."

"That would be great!"

"Thank you."

I was ecstatic and ran to Feng Qing's residence. A girl knocked on the door for me, asking for Feng Qing. The answer was, "She's not here". I hurried back to my dormitory and wrote a letter, saying:

Dear Feng Qing:

I accidentally saw you on the road just now, followed a short distance, and came here. Later, I learned from the phone that you live here, and I really have an indescribable joy in my heart.

If there was anything that made you unhappy in the past, please forgive me, and I solemnly apologize to you.

Please talk to me alone; if others are present, please protect me; people bully themselves first, and then others will bully them. This is a true truth that can stand the test.

It is not appropriate to describe to friends the various joys and sorrows encountered in the process of male and female communication; Talking too much can sometimes increase the rift between friendships. Because the essence of this kind of thing is owned by two people, and cannot be properly felt by a third party; This is my sincere suggestion. Wishing you a good sleep.

Sincerely,
Wang Wang

With the letter I had just written, I stepped up my pace and arrived at Feng Qing's rented house.

The landlord's son is in his twenties, and there are two girls standing next to him. They thought about it and said, "Feng Qing? Probably the one studying dance."

Feng Qing's bedroom had no lights, and the girl outside began to call out to her. The landlord's son walked out and politely said to me, "Please come in."

I walked into the room and the landlord's son found that Feng Qing was unresponsive. He turned to me and said, "She's not here."

I personally knocked on the door, but there was still no response. As a result, I took out a letter and said to the landlord's son: "I want to leave some messages and throw them under the door."

With a "card wipe" sound, the door opened, and Feng Qing, dressed in a light-yellow pajama with a gentle posture, gave me a charming smile - the kind that captivates me; But immediately closed the door again.

Normally, it would be difficult not to lose my soul for a while, but I immediately tried to wake up because the landlord's son was beside me.

"By the way, that's the one," I said politely to him. After finishing speaking, I lowered the letter through the door and whispered, "I'm leaving."

Before leaving, a landlady in her sixties walked out of the living room and pointed to a nearby reception room, saying kindly:

"If you come to find someone in the future, just sit here and wait. You're welcome."

"Thank you."

Returning to the dormitory, I walked back and forth on the rooftop square, gazing at the lights at the foot of the mountain alone and admiring the peaceful night view of Shamao Mountain on the other side. My mind was filled with Feng Qing's charming smile, and I truly realized what it was like to be "soulful". I prayed silently, requesting the blessings of the gods, agreeing that Feng Qing and I are the best couple, and praying for a blessing from heaven so that I can cherish her for a lifetime.

Unexpectedly, the atmosphere on the second night was completely different. After dinner, I arrived at Feng Qing's residence and found three landlords at home. In addition to the two I saw last night, there was also an old gentleman with an unusually cold attitude. They sat around the hall, only playing cards.

"She won't come back tonight," the landlady said coldly again. "She doesn't welcome you to look for her like this. You can't come here in the future. We can't let boys come here."

"We haven't had any unpleasant things, I'm good friends with her."

"She doesn't like you, she made it clear to me. As a man, why do you need to be like this?"

"May I ask when she moved here?"

"......" They were busy playing cards and didn't speak.

"Can you please tell me when she moved in?"

"A man!"

"Can you please tell me, because this is very important for my judgment."

"......" She still didn't say anything. Shake her head, look at the card, raise her hand and wave twice, asking me to leave.

I stood for a while and then said: "She may have misunderstood something for a moment. Her tantrum may be short-lived, please believe me."

"It's been half a year now; what kind of misunderstanding will make you confused? She's no longer dating you, man! Why worry about not finding a girl?"

"......" I couldn't say a word, just stood there in a daze.

"Her father brought her here and told us not to be disturbed."

"I only request your permission to come here in the future, okay? I won't cause harm to anyone, please rest assured."

"No, if you have anything to say, go to school to talk. You're not allowed to come here."

I walked back to my dormitory and wrote a short article titled "*Let me Be a Farming Ox*":

> The empty land,
> Peaceful and quiet.
> Growing among flowers and wild grass,
> I am a strong buffalo.
> Listen to the older generation say:
> "Being born into the mortal world is like being imprisoned.
> Forget it! What kind of dream is leisurely.
> coexist with human beings,
> How can we be allowed to pursue freedom?"
> "I am very resigned,
> Born with diligence.
> I am willing to cross the fields,
> I can help with agricultural income."
> Unfortunately,
> She is a bullfighter,
> At all,
> I have nothing against her.
> The wind and sand billowed in the field,
> Off the field, there were loud roars,

Today,

It is bound to force one party to shame.

Ha Jo! Ha Jo!

That red battle letter,

Make me

Irritating nostrils, tears streaming down.

Let her wake up, God!

Waste my nature in vain.

Actually, it is

Extremely gentle.

When will she spare me?

When will she spare me?

When will she make me one

farming ox?

After writing, I throw it into Feng Qing's school mailbox.

It was a starry night, and I walked to the high ground behind the red house, standing outside the wall to visit it. Every room was lit, and the room was quiet without any sound. There is a large road behind me, and occasionally sparse cars rush past.

I stood for a long time, helpless. Holding a short wooden stick in my hand, I wrote on the wall, "Feng Qing, Feng Qing……" and passed the time meaningless.

"It's too far, go to the front and have a look! Hopefully I won't run into the landlord." I thought as I walked.

The window in front was half open, and I was about to approach when suddenly a girl approached the window; I was taken aback and quickly squatted down, my heart pounding, feeling the meaning of the so-called 'To

die at the sight of light'. That is to say, at night, a person who behaves stealthily and improperly is so afraid and disgusted with the light!

The squatting posture didn't take a few steps, and the landlord's conversation was getting closer and closer to the door. I ran and crawled, crouching on the outside of the hedge next to the house.

The landlord turned on the headlights next to the house and came to wash the mop under the faucet. She said:

"These turfs need to be mowed."

"The weather has turned cold, and the grass grows slowly. But it's not beautiful without pruning."

"What is that?"

"Where? I can't see clearly in the dark." The landlord's son walked towards the tree.

"It seems to move."

"It's a plastic toy, someone threw it in from outside the wall, or it was blown in by the wind," he said as he picked up the toy and walked back.

After a while, the landlord handed his son a mop and said, "Don't forget to turn off the outside lights when you come in."

"Okay! I see." The landlord's son walked towards the hedge with a mop in his hand, and I was sweating profusely, almost fainting. Suddenly, he swung the mop over and draped it over the hedge, with water droplets dripping onto my head.

He walked into the room and turned off the exterior lights. My hair got wet and I walked back to school with a deflated look.

On November 22nd, I thought, "Feng Qing has gone up the mountain for accommodation. Do I still need to worry about my self-esteem and face? Why don't I go to the classroom to find her? Moreover, her landlord also said, 'If you have anything to say, go to school to talk.'" However, first of all, I must apologize to her classmates because I once scolded them at the roadside stall. In the morning, I got up and wrote a few brief apology words:

Dear Feng Qing:

If peonies bloom well, they also need the support of green leaves. Everyone needs friends. I envy your happy atmosphere.

The students in your class, in order to take care of you, do not hesitate to glare at me. If I wasn't too confused, I should be grateful to them. It's just my fault for being too impatient. Now, with a guilty and uneasy expression and heartfelt gratitude, I have come. Please convey these to them on my behalf.

In the afternoon, I will wait for you outside the door after class.

Sincerely,
Wang Wang

After writing it, I deliberately didn't seal the envelope and planned to deliver the letter in the first class in the morning and come to the classroom to find her in the afternoon.

The bell for the first class rang, and when I arrived at Room 401 of the Da Ren Guan, I found the classroom full, with men and women, clearly two classes merging into one.

The classmate by the door helped me notify Feng Qing, but instead, the door was closed as a result. It was Feng Qing who asked them to do this, with a smile on his face and a proud expression.

I opened the door, walked into the center of the classroom in full view, and handed the letter to Feng Qing. Feng Qing was a bit anxious and said first:

"I don't want to receive the letter." Take the book and sweep it to the ground.

The teacher is coming soon, I didn't expect the letter to be dropped to the ground, let alone have time to explain or apologize. I had to quickly withdraw and leave, thinking to myself, "After reading the letter, you know that the intention of this letter is only to apologize in advance, and I will only talk to you this afternoon."

A few minutes later, I looked over from the balcony and found out that Feng Qing was taking an exam. I have classes myself this morning. So, I walked to the opposite balcony and greeted my master's class classmates, then took out a book to read and prepared for my third English class.

Feng Qing walked out of the classroom and saw me standing on the balcony reading from a distance. She walked back to the classroom and brought the classmate who had the most heated argument with me last time by the stall. Feng Qing said to me, "What you have done has caused me disgust." He then returned the letter to me.

"Have you read it?" I took the letter back into my backpack, but in fact, it wasn't sealed. She should have read it. I said, "This is an apology to your classmates. I shouldn't have done that last time."

"If she is interested in you, she will also take the initiative to greet you on the way."

"I used to be really influenced, but now it's different. I have my own opinion. I'll tell you now that I don't like socializing with you."

"My classmates are nearby." I felt ashamed and whispered to her.

"How many times have I told you that I have no intention of dating you? You have been bothering me all along……"

Feng Qing spoke relentlessly and loudly, and I could only calmly accept the blame. I am the class representative and my grades are also very good. Two women and one man in my class, standing on the side of the balcony, finally personally learned that the rumors of the bullying I have suffered are true; But they all gave me face and deliberately made a conscious effort to read, and no one discussed or questioned Feng Qing with me afterwards.

Chapter 12   Third Party

As the publishing department was revising the Chinese dictionary, Leng Na, a younger sister from the university department, approached me and said, "Senior, I know your secret."

"What secret is it?"

"I live with that classmate from the dance department. How can you thank me?"

"Is it true?" I looked surprised.

"It's true. It's really a coincidence. I heard there are two dance majors living there, but I didn't expect it to be her. They're both quite cute."

"Have you mentioned me?"

"Not yet. I'm considering whether to tell her or not."

Previously, I had always believed that the essence of dating belonged to two people, and outsiders could not deeply appreciate the ups and downs involved; So, I rarely discuss various situations of my love with outsiders. Just because I talk less, in everyone's eyes, my current situation will also appear

much calmer. Now, Leng Na suddenly moved out of the school dormitory and became Feng Qing's roommate. I'm afraid all the difficulties I've encountered before will be exposed. At this moment, my mood couldn't help but sink.

On the fifth day, Leng Na told me that another dance roommate was named Xiao Mei. Leng Na will continue to work overtime in the publishing department tonight, while I only work during the day. Leng Na said to me:

"Senior, there is no need to look for Feng Qing at night. She will spend the night with her classmates in Beiyelu (the name of the building). If she is not in Bayelu, she will go back to Gongguan; because she is afraid that you will harass her."

Since that's the case, I didn't visit Feng Qing at night. The next day, at two o'clock in the afternoon, I was walking along the road to Feng Qing's residence when I met Leng Na, who was about to go to work. She asked:

"Senior, where are you going."

"Go find her. "

"She's not here, there's no need to go."

I have to turn back halfway. In the evening, I called Gongguan and Feng Qing's younger cousin answered the phone. Her attitude completely changed:

"Feng Qing said that your attitude is too radical, causing her disgust; this matter is no longer possible, and I would like to suggest that you find another girl."

"Your attitude is too different from the previous few days. I have suffered a lot of injustice, do you know? She said I am too confident, and I think I never dare to be too confident or arrogant. The first day I approached her, she had a good attitude and even smiled. However, the next day, I was ignored by the landlord, and they all ignored me and focused on playing cards. When I refused to leave, she said some irritating words and refused to allow me to go to her place in the future. One after another, Feng Qing's approach was clearly to create opportunities for others to intervene, which could easily lead to branching out, didn't she know? She didn't think about it. The landlord's son is about the same age as me, and she even authorized him to drive me away."

"This really hurts you a lot," she softened her tone.

"I dare not go to her residence to find her because I dare not act recklessly, and the landlord will drive me away. I dare not go to the classroom to find her because she doesn't even give face. Only you can help, could you please do me a favor?"

"We used to see that you were quite pitiful. We helped you talk a lot, but she didn't listen, and I think it was useless." After a pause, she added: "I have told her many times, but to no avail. Her mother also tried to persuade her, and her cousin also tried to persuade her, but she didn't listen........" Her words became increasingly incomprehensible and ambiguous, making it difficult for me to understand. Finally, with a "stuck" sound, she hung up the phone; Leave me standing there with my mind full of doubts.

Chapter 13 Swearing

The Shilin Theater is currently staging the old film "Liang Zhu". Leng Na suggested that she call on several students working in the publishing department to watch it together after work. Except for another male student from the literary institute and me, all the others are female students. Watching the movie together, I also find it interesting.

On the noon of December 9th, I walked to Feng Qing's residence and rang the electric bell. Leng Na walked out and stood by the door, saying in an awkward tone of "unbelievable" and "guilty":

"She's not here. Senior, how could you come here?"

"……" I looked at that embarrassing expression, as if I had accidentally broken into the men's restricted area, and suddenly felt ashamed." I come here as I had no choice but come to see her. Since she is not here, I have to go back."

I went straight to the publishing department and asked a junior sister to come to the hallway:

"Will Leng Na come this afternoon?"

"She has classes and cannot come."

"Do you know why she recently moved out of the school dormitory?"

"……" She smiled mysteriously.

"Why on earth?"

"She's in a bad mood. Change her environment! You go to the classroom to find Yiti. They used to live together, and she knows better."

I used my break time to find Yiti and said, "Can you tell me why Leng Na moved out of the school dormitory?"

"Because she has recently been abandoned by her boyfriend and is in a bad mood, when she sees us having a partner, she becomes jealous and difficult to get along with."

"Who is that boy?"

"It's Wang Ri."

"Is it him?"

"You don't know?"

"Yes, I never knew." I thanked Yiti for telling me this, and I was extremely nervous inside. When I walked back to the literary institute, a senior told me:

"I heard that Feng Qing's mother hopes she will marry a doctor in the future. Her classmates are all laughing at you, saying that the letter you wrote is very '...... that'; Feng Qing has already circulated your letter to them."

I returned to my dormitory and decided to put all my eggs in one basket, writing a letter:

Dear Feng Qing:

Someone told Miss A, "He is very sick with lovesickness and will die soon." Miss A replied, "If he really means it, he should prove it with death." Then what do you think of Miss A?

Your elder cousin always harshly blame me: "What is the definition of your 'last time'." To be honest, I have nothing to say. Have you ever thought about how this dilemma of 'breaking promises' came about?

Several younger students said, "Leng Na has been abandoned by someone boy, so she will be jealous of those who have partners." This shocking news made me feel restless. She once said in a very critical tone: "Senior, how could you come here?" (referring to your residence)

I have been severely injured, so stop here and the effort I have given you is already impeccable. On December 23rd, I will personally come to you once, and I need your smile and kindness; If it fails, then this is the true 'last time' and we will not interact with each other in the future. If I break my promise, I am willing to be struck by thunder and lightning from the heavens. The gods are above, and they can testify for me.

Sincerely,
Wang Wang

Leng Na's attitude makes me feel worried. If Feng Qing is not forced to talk, it seems that the whole thing will be messed up. Therefore, on December 10th, I submitted this letter. From this point in time, Feng Qing has a two-week consideration period; At that time, she must decide whether to socialize or break off.

Chapter 14　Two Weeks

After receiving the tip off letter, Feng Qing saw me from a distance on the road and hurriedly led a classmate to flee in panic. I think the 'contemplation period' requires her to think calmly, so I don't care about her reaction. Moreover, I am willing to take advantage of this "consideration period" to express more personal thoughts, so I wrote two letters:

First letter:

Dear Feng Qing:

Since I met you, I have invested a considerable amount of time and effort, which has had a significant impact on my studies; I just hope you can treat me politely as soon as possible, so that I can turn resistance into assistance and catch up in terms of grades.

I once thought, do dancers in their fifties and sixties have the ability to compete with so-called "rising stars" in their twenties and thirties in dance art? Is it possible for her to expect warm applause and concern from society again? This is a life that is almost like 'flowers blooming and withering'. The achievements on paper are completely different, as the older one gets, the more fruitful their achievements may be; As a result, one receives more and more courtesy and respect, which is the life of 'cultivating the right fruit'. So, in your spare time practicing dance, I would like to encourage you to enter the library more and study relevant written materials. I am willing to help you.

Sincerely,

Wang Wang.

It's so hard to write this letter under a big tree, fighting against the wind for paper!

Second letter:

December 13th, 1982

Dear Feng Qing:

The passionate man, the passionate man,

Laugh at your absurd behavior,

Miss beauty, beauty is far away on the water side.

Thinking in the morning, thinking in the evening,

At the sight of spring suburban green, suddenly

chrysanthemum yellow,

Helpless, beauty always hides her heart.

Now I......

On a winter night, trapped in a bed of sorrow,

Unable to get rid of it, my heart is almost crazy,

I can no longer say how strong I have always been.

Look at this year

On the way to Huagang Road,

Birds are silent, flowers are not fragrant;

The gods know that my heart is sad,

Heartbroken,

Worry lingers all day,

like the entanglement of the intestines.

I once explored the western chamber late at night,

The cold stars and bright moon shine brightly against each
other.
Lone geese have wings but cannot fly,
Gold and jade complement each other,
Whisper to the beauty,
Your innocent heart
How long do you want me to wait?
It's no longer cold.
My heart is lost,
Trying to ask you:
With a small boat,
Will I be able to cross the river?

Sincerely,
Wang Wang

On the morning of December 15th, while working in the publishing department, Leng Na walked up to me and said, "Senior, please go outside for a moment."

I followed her out, and she handed me a letter…… the letter I wrote to Feng Qing on December 9. The content included whistle-blowing and self-cursing. She looked very solemn and said:

"Senior, you wrote this letter."

"Did Feng Qing show you this letter?" I was shocked and almost fainted; Wrinkling brows, I took the letter over.

"Hmm! Feng Qing said, 'You've been saying good things about Wang Wang, but he's writing to scold you.' So, she showed it to me."

"……" I gasped for breath, feeling extremely weak; For a moment, I didn't know what to say.

"I told Feng Qing that your idea is really childish. Could it be that when I see someone else having a partner, am I really jealous of them? Last night when I read the letter, my whole body trembled and I couldn't speak with anger. Feng Qing kept saying sorry to me." Leng Na was extremely sad, panting, out of breath. And then she said: "Anyway, even if I really make a mistake, you shouldn't publicize it to the public. Moreover, is it acceptable to say 'abandoned by a boy'? What is 'abandonment'? Who is that boy you're talking about?"

"It's Wang Ri, I heard someone say it." I saw her so sad and instinctively thought she was really innocent, and at the same time, I blamed her wrongly.

"Nonsense, who said he is my boyfriend?"

"......" I can't answer anything.

"I told Feng Qing that this kind of thing cannot be fabricated by you out of thin air. You wrote about 'Several younger students', who and who are they?"

"It was said by one person, because everyone else looked mysterious, I thought their speeches were consistent."

"Who is that person? She shouldn't be spreading rumors."

I took a breath and said, "It's Yang Yiti."

"I knew it was her."

"I want to retract this letter."

"No way. It's already Feng Qing's property and I must return it to her. She was very sad last night and said she hurt me. She kept apologizing to me and I said I appreciate her showing me the letter."

I was greatly surprised by Feng Qing's behavior. Being alone in the dormitory, my mood was in turmoil and I couldn't help but write a letter to blame:

December 15th, 1982

Feng Qing:

In front of a friend with polio, I don't mention the great benefits of running; In front of a friend with a broken finger, I don't show off my gold ring; In front of a friend who was heartbroken by a breakup, I don't say how happy my love was, this is compassion. When I tell you what happened to her, don't I hope you will develop this spirit? Besides, people's hearts are unpredictable. I remind you to take precautions. What's wrong? Others did tell me this, and I candidly conveyed it to you based on my trust in you; And I hope you have a tacit understanding. And your actions are the most unforgivable.

I know maybe she has been trying to put in good words for me all along. Even if I have misunderstandings about her, I hope to resolve it in the future because of our conversation. Who expected you to publish the letter.

I was supposed to see you on the 23rd, but I think we can cancel it now.

Wang Wang

After submitting the letter, it was only two short days. Somehow, my anger had subsided, and I felt that I had put in a lot of effort for a long time. It would be a pity to give up easily; I also feel regretful about the letter I wrote the day before yesterday. Therefore, I wrote another letter to inform Feng Qing that I will no longer consider the incident of the last public letter and will continue to go as scheduled on December 23rd.

On the morning of the 20th, Leng Na was in the publishing department, looking for a male student from the literary institute and me, as well as several classmates from the university department. They said that they would hold a birthday party for a certain student in the evening, and suggested that the cake should be bought by me and another senior who is studying at the Graduate School. The other food should be shared by the students from the university department. Since everyone is so enthusiastic, I obliged without hesitation.

Around 6 pm, eight classmates attended and sang birthday songs together, talking and laughing. Halfway through the meal, Wang Ri suddenly arrived at the meeting. He usually didn't interact with the group, but now he even came for a drink and had a great conversation with Leng Na. Leng Na enthusiastically said to me:

"January 19th is my birthday, and I promise to keep Feng Qing. Could you please buy a cake for me, senior? Our venue can be used, and perhaps even a ball can be held."

"But……, I can't dance." I felt a little embarrassed.

"Can't dance, just watch from the sidelines!"

"Did Feng Qing say anything to you? "

"She said you're stupid. She said you're the first boy he knows since he entered college; before that, she would be shy when she met a boy, but you scared her; your attitude was very wrong. Even if she had a good impression of you, she couldn't bear your terrible behavior."

"I haven't looked for her in the classroom for a long time, and I don't know what to do properly. I don't think there's anything terrible about my behavior."

"She said you always say she's good, but she thinks she's not good. You may just think too well of her just because you didn't get it. So, even if you get her in the future, what's the point."

"Since she has such concerns, why does she always evade? She doesn't give me the opportunity to get to know and see her clearly; saying that kind of thing is a bit self contradictory."

"Senior, Feng Qing said that on the afternoon of December 23rd, she is willing to take a walk outside with you. You must not scare her."

"Really? That must be, it must be." I was overjoyed and speechless."

I am both looking forward to and delighted to learn in advance that Feng Qing is willing to talk to me. On the 21st, I wrote again to remind Feng Qing.

Dear Feng Qing:

Talking to you alone is something I have been longing for a long time, and I believe you can understand my feelings. I wish I could come to your residence every day, but the cold landlord may stop me. I wish I could call you every day, but you always don't answer.

I have sworn and cursed myself. Perhaps that was an "inappropriate" behavior, and while I regret it, I also want to ask for your forgiveness. December 23rd is my only opportunity, possibly the most severe blow, or an indescribable joy. Everything is in your hands. Please, please.

Sincerely,
Wang Wang

Chapter 15   Termination

On the afternoon of December 23rd, I confidently went to find Feng Qing. The dance classroom only had a small opening, and a girl walked up to the door and said to me, "Feng Qing didn't come to class today."

"......" I felt disappointed and immediately rushed to her residence, but still couldn't find her trace. I was puzzled and thought to myself, "Why did she suddenly change her mind? causing trouble again!" I felt a bit angry and walked into the store to buy something.

I didn't take the usual path and walked around to the sports ground. Just around the corner, I found Feng Qing and a group of girls sitting in a shop after class, preparing to eat. She was wearing a purple tight-fitting outfit - no different from her previous "long conversation".

As I approached, Feng Qing said, "I don't want to talk to you."

"I don't want to talk now either." I was very calm and turned to leave, holding the item I just purchased in my hand.

Mr. Zhang Qiyun, the founder of the University, had previously served as the Minister of Education. After he founded the school, he accommodated many honorary uncles who guarded various buildings or were responsible for campus cleaning work; Da Ren Guan also has a resident uncle, but his dialect is very unique and difficult to understand. I have been a student here for a long time, and naturally, he recognizes me. Sometimes, he would confide in me some of his inner words, although most of them were incomprehensible, in order to sympathize with his experiences, I often stopped to listen to him speak for a while, sharing some of the "depression" that had accumulated in his heart for a long time.

That day, as I walked past the classroom building, the honorary uncle appeared in front of me again. I was in a state of weakness and was stopped by him. The uncle said vigorously, "...... Ma Gai...... Ma Gai...... squad leader...... Communist Party...... battalion commander...... shot dead......" As he spoke, he lifted one foot so high, pretending to fall, and then stood up, laughing non-stop.

I tilted my head and leaned against the wall, expressionless. After taking a deep breath, I said, "Uncle, I happen to have something to do today and can't chat with you. I'm really sorry." I bowed and turned to leave.

The melancholy night, the dead silent earth. I closed the door tightly and wrote two letters, the first one:

Dear Feng Qing:

> Why? Why?
> Stack after stack, all of them
> An annoying storm.
> It must be heaven's jealousy of me.
> See your beauty,
> See your tenderness,
> See your heart blooming.
> On December 23rd,
> Expect to play the song of triumph,
> It makes me feel even sadder.
> Waiting for you,
> To the gods
> Detailed explanation.
>
> Feng Qing!
> Since ancient times, good deeds have been tormented,
> I knew earlier
> This is a
> A difficult river to cross.
> Do not shed tears,
> Do not lock your eyebrows,
> Fate stirs people's anger,
> Waiting for us both,
> Break it with sincerity.
> Feng Qing!
> Please think twice,
> Between your words and actions,

It will be decided that,

Do I become

A moth pouncing on the torch.

Second letter:

Dear Feng Qing:

Writing this letter in the middle of the night, you know, my heart is breaking.

I am certain of your attitude, so I am struggling recklessly. Perhaps tonight, you are as unstable as me. Avoidance has become your sin, don't you know? It really shouldn't be. Think about it, how many times have you been reminded?

If you had originally intended to socialize with me, now only if you confess yourself can it count, right? I'm really at a loss. If you call, it might not be too late.

Sincerely,

Wang Wang

I don't want to give up until I understand the matter. On December 28th, I went to Feng Qing's residence and Xiao Mei came out and said, "Feng Qing is not here."

"I want to talk to her in person. May I ask when she will be here?"

"I don't know, then, why don't you come every day!"

"Okay," I decided to go every day until she appeared.

Unexpectedly, the next morning while I was working, Leng Na handed me a plump letter and said, "Senior, your letter."

"Thank you!" I took the letter and tore open a small opening, only to find that it was filled with fragments of paper. I closed my mouth tightly, put the letter in my pocket, and continued working, pretending to be okay. Leng Na felt very serious and didn't bother to say a word, burying herself in her work.

After working for half an hour, I walked to an empty corner and opened the letter. Many of the letters I wrote to Feng Qing have been torn to pieces, and Feng Qing has attached another letter:

December 29th, 1982

Wang Wang:

Please don't harass me in any way, otherwise, go to the announcement board and enjoy your work. For the last cautious warning, I have already said what I should have said. We have no connection at all, and you don't need to explain anymore. I don't care if you exist or not. Please take care of yourself and not hinder yourself or harm others.

ps. I reluctantly wrote to you out of pity, otherwise, don't blame me for being rude to you.

Feng Qing

In my eyes, Feng Qing's various actions only seem to me to be "Unclear organization and constantly changing" and unreasonable. I don't care what the outcome is, I must see her in person. So, that night, I still visited once, and Leng Na answered the door and said, "Feng Qing is not here."

"Okay, I will come again tomorrow."

The next day, on November 16th of the lunar calendar, I walked under the moonlight, just wanting to know the reason for Feng Qing's drastic change in attitude. I rang the doorbell and asked for Feng Qing. A girl turned around and went into the room to invite her. I walked back to the main road and waited, and saw Feng Qing and a boy walking out of the room. The man was tall and at least 180 centimeters tall; Feng Qing was dressed in bright red. It is an atmosphere of resolute and solemn silence, shedding blood and tears; One step of hatred and one step of regret, she was as cold as ice; Finally, two people were side by side in front of me, and I said:

"This is……"

"He is my friend."

"Actually…… she had already told me about it…… I didn't expect it to take so long." His expression was coy and unnatural, with a slight smile. I think he is such a guilty conscience and incompetent "actor".

"What do you have to say?" Feng Qing's face was serious.

"No, I just came to see you once."

"Actually, this kind of thing……"

"Enough, goodbye." I interrupted her speech, bowed, and then left.

The north wind is fierce, the earth is sorrowful, and I lazily stroll back to my bedroom.

The streets of Taipei are exceptionally lively, with over a dozen pedestrians forming a semicircle by the roadside to watch others hawk things. I also went to watch. The young seller was holding a clapper and shouting at the top of his lungs:

"1500, is there anyone else to shout?"

"1550."

"1600, do you still have one? To be honest, 1700 is not enough to buy the foot of this statue."

"Young man," A deep voice called me to the side. I took a closer look and saw that it was a strong man. He whispered: "Please leave if you don't want to buy."

"How do you know I'm not buying?"

"Do you want to buy?…… which one?"

" I just came here; how do I know which one I want?"

"I know you won't buy it, please go!" The rough man poked my elbow.

"How can they all see it?" I protested in confusion.

"They want to buy it; you don't want to buy it."

There were several accomplices not far behind him, all looking at me with wide eyes; I swaggered away with a fire burning in my stomach.

Passing by the entrance of the theater, I stopped to look at the poster and spent 150 yuan to go in and watch the show.

The venue was packed to capacity, and I stood on the right side of the stage with my back against the wall. There are more and more people standing, and the crowd is unbearable. The entire theater was filled with smoke and the air was very foul.

The young ladies who came on stage were all stripped off and covered themselves with a shawl. Big-name celebrities wore white transparent clothes and sang the Minnan language song "Can't Wait for Someone".

"Come on, I need to find an audience." The host took a microphone, took a few steps forward, pointing to the man in red in the middle of the first row. He announced to the audiences, "This brother bought a monthly ticket and has been sitting in the seat of the Foundation God since three o'clock in the afternoon. Now I want to invite him to come to the stage and worship the womb queen, so that he can have a smooth career and make a lot of money after he returns. Come on, please stand up!"

The audience in red happily walked onto the stage, and the host had already prepared a young lady to lie there, waiting for him to visit. Under the watchful gaze of the crowd, he was asked to put on a posture of prostrate kowtow and diligent death penalty, which made him feel embarrassed and caused constant laughter from the audiences. The host then said:

There was an old gentleman who was taking a bus. When he wanted to get off, he saw the bus pass by without stopping. He immediately argued with the lady in charge of the bus and said, "Hey, hello, miss, why don't you have 'beep'?" She said, "I have 'beep'." "Your 'beep' is too small." "My beep' is very big."

"Nowadays, movie stars don't get old and never see wrinkles on their faces. Why? Because they often go for skin pulling surgery, which involves cutting some skin under their foreheads, tightening the skin underneath, and sewing it up to eliminate wrinkles. Later on, the navel may run to the neck. Therefore, some people advised Apipo, said: 'Apipo, you can't have any more facelifts. If you do, you will grow a beard.'"

Chapter 16   Suspicious

When I suffered a severe blow and was at my lowest mood, Leng Na showed full sympathy and warmth. I walked shoulder to shoulder with her on campus. She said:

"Senior, why did you have an unpleasant argument with Feng Qing for the first time."

"She said that her family was opposed to her dating me. As a result of my own speculation and reflection, I felt that I should not describe my family as if it were a poor family, so I wrote to her to tell her about my family situation; her attitude was once obviously getting better. However, I hurt her by writing a letter in a daze. She thought I was expressing blame, so she got angry."

"Now Feng Qing has a boyfriend from Qingda, whom I have also seen. He is very tall. On the day before Christmas, their class held a ball and they had to attend with their partner. He also went there."

"......" I remained silent.

"Feng Qing once cried because she received your letter. She thought you had caused her a lot of trouble. Several classmates in her class came to comfort her, and someone advised her to tear up the letter and return it. Their words are very unfavorable to you, and I cannot scold you together with them; there was no choice but to listen quietly."

"A long time ago, she said she had a boyfriend, but I never believed it, so I tried and tried again. Now that it has been confirmed that she has a boyfriend, I certainly don't need to worry about this matter anymore. If it had been confirmed before, there's no need to drag it on until now." After a while, I said again, "She said she had a boyfriend from Taiwan University before, how did he become a Qingda's?"

"I saw him, he really comes from Qingda." Leng Na said again: "Senior, when she heard that your family has money, her attitude changed. Do you want this kind of girl?"

"At that time, I felt a bit regretful, but later I felt that it wasn't her fault; in fact, I should be mostly responsible. Oh, by the way, you are roommates and you must get along, but don't misunderstand her behavior due to my influence. In fact, after the unpleasant incident that occurred last semester, she said she wanted to take a break from school. I said if she took a break, I would also take a break with her, which helped her calm down. She is really not a girl who only cares about money, I can trust this."

"No, no. After listening to what you said, coupled with my own observations and judgments, I know she won't be that kind of person. I'm a bit worried that what I said earlier may make you mistakenly think they are the kind of bad people, but in fact, they are all very innocent."

On January 10, 1983, Leng Na said to me and another senior at the literary institute, "Senior, you have already said that you want to celebrate my birthday on the 19th. Can you hold it early? The school girls said they have final exams and will be very busy then."

"You said last time that you hoped everyone would come to the place where you live to help you hold a birthday party."

"No, our landlord doesn't want miscellaneous people to come in for a birthday party, afraid of hindering others from studying. Therefore, I want to borrow Yaya's dormitory for the celebration."

I and two classmates from the literature research institute are responsible for buying cakes, while other college students buy soda, snacks, and so on. Half an hour into the activity, a student asked me, "Senior, how is Feng Qing's situation now?"

"It's over. Recently, my family will arrange for me to go back for a blind date."

"Senior," Leng Na said, "Feng Qing knows that you are going to help me celebrate my birthday tonight. Before I went out, she said she wanted to eat fresh milk cake. Please cut a piece off first, and I will take it back to her to eat later."

"......" I was surprised and then a little uneasy, saying, "They didn't sell fresh milk cakes. I didn't originally buy cream, but the boss arranged the order receipts, so I had to place an order."

"It's okay, they're all delicious."

I took the lead in cutting a piece and handed it to Leng Na.

On January 29th, while working in the publishing department, Leng Na said to the girl next to her in a moderate volume, "All the girls in the dance department have moved out."

After five minutes, I walked forward and asked, "Feng Qing moved away? Why?"

"Her mother wants her to move back because there is no one living in Gongguan." Leng Na said after a while, "She sent me photos and wrote inscriptions. I am very moved."

I'm not interested, just focused on my work. After work, Leng Na found a few girls and went to chat with my classmates at the literature institute, watching TV, and eating snacks; Afterwards, they also approached me to join the conversation.

Leng Na changed the topic and said with a hint of regret, "Senior, I wanted to show you the photo of Feng Qing, but I forgot."

"What does it do?" I really feel dull and uninteresting.

On the morning of January 31st, while working in the publishing department, Leng Na walked up to me and said, "Senior, the guy you saw last time was actually not Feng Qing's boyfriend. He was a student in the architecture department of our school. You have a misunderstanding about Feng Qing, and I want to find time to talk to you."

Despite that, after work, Leng Na quickly left and ate on her own for three consecutive days, always mysterious. On the fourth day, Leng Na and I had dinner together. At the beginning, we were silent and almost finished eating, Leng Na said:

"Senior, at first you were too straight forward. She was scared by you, that's why she was so troublesome."

"……" I seem to have heard too much and am too lazy to explain.

"Feng Qing said that you described her too well, but in fact, she is not that good; If you find out after you two marry that she is not as you think, you will definitely be disappointed; So, she decided to stop dating you."

"What is this nonsense? Everyone has shortcomings, and so do I. How could I ask her to be perfect?"

"Alas! You are all too much……"

"Did we do anything too outrageous?"

"It seems that you and she have each insisted on something. I don't know what you are insisting on. But you really have a misunderstanding about her."

"I always keep a low voice; how can I persist for anything?" After a while, I said, "I once lost my temper with her, but later felt regretful and would immediately correct it."

As soon as I finished eating, Leng Na immediately handed over the fragrant tissue with a very gentle attitude.

Chapter 17   Playing Basketball

Leng Na borrowed basketball from the Literature Research Institute from me. In the evening, she always wears hot pants and stockings, sitting on the concrete steps next to the stadium reading, while basketball is provided for some unfamiliar classmates to shoot; Two or three basketballs were playing

non-stop on the field. The road next to the stadium is a must-have for me to go out for dinner. I always have to greet her and even walk into the stadium to practice throwing a few balls. Afterwards, we went to dinner together. After finishing her meal, she often pays first. I couldn't help but believe that her strange behavior was related to Feng Qing.

One day, when walking across the campus, a school girl said mockingly, "Senior, Leng Na wears hot pants and silk stockings to play basketball with you, and she's very coquettish, isn't she?" Her words sounded sour.

"Don't think crooked, it's nothing."

Ever since Feng Qing and Leng Na met, Leng Na and I often had meals together and walked together on campus. This special scene has caused the students to look puzzled and rumors have spread. I thought to myself: If it weren't related to Feng Qing, why should I be so close to Leng Na? In recent days, Leng Na's behavior has been mysterious and strange, and she is quite attentive. Occasionally, she also reveals that she is carrying information from Feng Qing's side. Seeing how hard she is working, I have even more doubts about whether Feng Qing is actually playing any tricks. After returning to the dormitory, I wrote a short paragraph in my diary:

> Feng Qing, do you really have such a heart? You always emphasize that you already have a boyfriend. If it's just for fun, I don't care. But I have already sworn, how could you have such cruel behavior! At that most critical moment, you had the heart to treat me like this, how could you not make me feel heartbroken!
>
> For the sake of a woman, I don't even think about my parents. Will they forgive me? Can my sin be forgiven? Until now, even if I can repair the sores in front of my eyes, I must gouge out the flesh of my heart!
>
> Feng Qing, I can feel that it seems like you were willing to socialize before. Who was playing tricks on you? Who is blocking it? Who is destroying it? It's fate, it's it that sets up a hard iron wall that keeps me shouting through the window.

If you are willing to reveal the truth and tell me that your heart has always belonged to me, then I will deal with the magic of fate to the end and never yield. It is Li Shangyin who said, "Silkworms in spring will stop spinning silk when they die, and candles will stop weeping when they are burned to ashes."

I believe the gods are compassionate, and the true love in the world is really rare. I pray that the gods can see the level of our hearts and know that we have long been deeply intertwined.

When the golden wind and jade dew meet, they surpass countless others in the world. How could it be: the golden wind floats frequently, and the jade dew always ignores it!

Subsequently, I wrote to Feng Qing again, but Feng Qing still ignored me. I called and her family became more patient. Her mother said:

"Wang, you are a promising young man. You can find someone better than Feng Qing. She already has a boyfriend, and we don't want to see her in trouble again."

Later, I called again, and Feng Qing answered. I said:

"Why don't you talk to me in person?"

"I don't think it's necessary. I've already made it clear to you that I should say. I already have a boyfriend who will be engaged after graduation. He often comes to my house. Please don't bother me anymore."

"You keep saying you have a boyfriend, so why didn't you write a letter to refuse me before?"

"I don't think it's necessary to reply to the letter."

"Why did you suddenly move up the mountain in the beginning?"

"Can't I move up the mountain? I'm just doing my homework, but you're telling people this everywhere?"

"So, why did you open the door and smile when I came to Shanzai Hou to find you?"

"I feel very sad talking to you; please, don't, call, again," Feng Qing was furious, speaking word by word through gritted teeth, and then hung up the phone.

Leng Na seemed to be interested in playing basketball. She told me that she was going to buy a new ball and return it to the Literature Institute, and she wanted to keep the old one for herself. I advised her to have a new ball and just return the old one to the Literature Institute, but she refused. She said she already had feelings for the old ball.

After playing ball, we had dinner together. After the meal, sit on the grass. I say it bluntly:

"Recently, there have been many rumors. Someone asked me, 'Why didn't you have dinner with Leng Na today?' Some people laughed at me and said, 'Someone wears stockings to play basketball with you in the evening.' I feel the pressure of the rumors and can't bear it anymore."

"……" Leng Na only focused on eating fruits and didn't want to explain.

"Have you met Feng Qing recently?"

"I often see her, and every time I see her, she is very happy." After a while, she said, "Senior, will you hit your wife in the future?"

"Of course I won't hit my wife, nor will I scold my wife; if she really makes a mistake, I can just remind her when no one else is around."

"Xiao Mei's riding boots are at the Dazhuang Restaurant. If you want to chat with Feng Qing, I can call and ask her to notify Xiao Mei to come and pick them up. Oh, by the way, is there anything you want me to ask her on the phone for you?"

"……" I looked up at the night sky, feeling a bit tired, and then said, "Just don't mention it." After a few minutes, I said, "I'm a bit curious. Has Feng Qing raised the issue of the name strokes I mentioned?"

"Senior, you can't ask someone to change her name and strokes. Now is not the time to talk about getting married."

"I know I shouldn't have told her about that. But there are books like this on the market in Taiwan that make Taiwanese people afraid not to cooperate with those good or bad things. It may just be a form of seeking peace of mind, and we can't judge. It was my sister who mentioned to my mother that Feng Qing's name has a total of twenty strokes, saying that its characteristic is a "dilemma". I argued hard with my sister for a while, and then she stopped insisting and just said it was up to me. My family no longer cares about the issue of name strokes, but Feng Qing and I still can't come to an agreement. Last time, she told me: As soon as she graduates, she will get engaged. Now her boyfriend often comes to her house. Is it true?"

"Feng Qing is so cute! She always lied to you at first."

"What happened later?"

"The boyfriend she had when she was moving down the mountain last semester was real."

"……"These words sound confusing.

"It's okay not to mention it, it will always be a beautiful memory in the future."

"What beautiful memories?" I didn't want to talk anymore, stood up and said, "Let's go, it's time to go back."

After a few steps, Leng Na said, "Senior, don't think about her anymore. Your wife will be so pitiful in the future! You always think of Feng Qing."

"Can it be like this?" I couldn't help but get angry and hit the ball hard on the asphalt road, making a loud sound.

Passing through the store area, Leng Na said, "Let's go in and watch the ball."

"If you want to play, you can continue borrowing, why buy it?"

"No, I want to buy one and return it to the literary institute."

After watching the ball, she said to the boss, "Five hundred yuan, okay, I'll buy it the day after tomorrow." I just watched, too lazy to say another word. Walking to the side of the field, Leng Na said, "The weather is really nice. I only pitched for five minutes in the evening, and now I need to pitch a few more balls. You can go in."

"Okay, goodbye." I walked back to the dormitory alone.

Chapter 18   New Semester

It's the beginning of another new semester, and I no longer think about Feng Qing. I just want to let it fade away naturally. But Leng Na came again and said, "A few days ago, my brother sent me a box of oranges, and I specifically took them to deliver to Feng Qing. She was very happy."

"Oh!" I looked uninterested.

"This morning, I met her again. She ran over happily and said she wanted to practice dancing. I said I would call her tonight."

During my working hours, I focused on writing and remained silent for half a day. Leng Na told her classmates behind my back, "Our senior misses Feng Qing all day. It's so pitiful, he's too obsessed."

"Aren't you helping him? That's what the senior told us."

"It's not as easy as that. Both of them have strong personalities and have many family opinions, which makes things more complicated and difficult to explain for a while."

In the evening, I called Leng Na and asked, "Did you say you want to call Feng Qing tonight?"

"I did."

"What did she say?"

"It's better to talk outside, it's not convenient to talk on the phone."

So, I visited Leng Na, and we walked towards the school and sat on the cement steps of the basketball court.

"What did Feng Qing say just now?"

"I really regret meeting both of you. It doesn't matter if I just meet one of you," Leng Na said, laughing uncontrollably and adding, "You probably owed her too much in your previous life, that's why you're like this in this life."

I saw her smile and followed her silly smile, saying, "Maybe, I can't remember, maybe there was a credit loan problem in my previous life." But I quickly turned serious and asked, "What did she say just now?"

"I said I shouldn't have mentioned that fake boyfriend, but Feng Qing said, 'It doesn't matter if you say it, and you can tell him that I already have a boyfriend named ○○○.'"

"Is that all you talk about?" My face changed.

"Yes, she wants me to say that."

"If it's just for these words, you would have just told me on the phone. Why go so far?"

"Feng Qing said that if you really like her, you should bless her."

"Sure! I know she's a good person, and of course I'm willing to bless her."

"In fact, these things will become beautiful memories for you in the future."

"What kind of beautiful memories?" I couldn't help but feel angry and said, "Can it be called a beautiful memory? The whole thing is inexplicable, and my mind seems to be stuffed with a bunch of messy things."

"Feng Qing said you are too confident. Do you hold yourself up high? And you are very confident."

"This is a different matter. Blindly praising oneself may be arrogant; As for confidence, it is something that everyone needs. How can one shrink back from doing things and admit defeat when encountering small setbacks? Does Feng Qing like a man without confidence?" After a moment of silence, I said, "Actually, to be honest, I believe that it is natural for man and woman to socialize and even get married, and there is no need to force them, nor is there such a difficult thing as 'chasing a girlfriend'. At the beginning, I saw her as just a freshman and didn't want her to be pursued by me in just three or two days. I did have a heart to leave beautiful memories for her, and was willing to accept her series of blows and torments. I think she can also feel my intentions. It seems that we used to be able to communicate spiritually. However, it's strange that in the end, the whole thing changed and she became increasingly outrageous, which made me have to admit that I had to self examine. Maybe I was really wrong from the beginning. Perhaps she is not the kind of girl I imagined."

"That's right! I also told Feng Qing that my senior was not unreasonable. If she hadn't made some ambiguous remarks in the beginning, my senior wouldn't have behaved like this. But Feng Qing said she didn't, and she only talked to you once, without any connection." Leng Na added, "Later, they were all scolding you, but I didn't dare to tell you, for fear that you would suspect that I was also causing trouble."

"In her mind, perhaps only doctors are the best. It's okay, I believe there will still be my confidants in my level."

"She didn't mean that."

A few days later, I was reading in the library when a school girl came to ask a question with a book, and I was explaining it to her. Leng Na appeared and said:

"Senior, I've always been invited by you. I'm sorry, what do you want me to treat you tonight?"

"……" I scanned with a puzzled look, as the phrase "always being invited by you" was really nonsense. On the contrary, she often rushed to pay more than me.

As soon as it was time to get off work, dozens of students participating in work-study programs left the publishing department one after another. Leng Na appeared from the front, back, right, or left, and always appeared unexpectedly. I felt puzzled: "How come there are so many 'coincidences'?"

In terms of accommodation, since Feng Qing moved away, Leng Na invited another part-time student from the publishing department, Xia Huan,

to come in as a roommate. After living for a while, they were picky about this and that, so they made an appointment to go to Shilin at the foot of the mountain to find a house and also paid a deposit. On the day of the move, Leng Na asked Xia Huan to move down the mountain first. She told Xia Huan, "Senior Wang Wang is coming to move me, and I will be there soon."

That afternoon, I was indeed asked by her to come and help. Entering the room, feeling empty, I asked, "Where's the landlord?"

"The landlord is not here."

"Do you usually have such freedom in and out?" I walked around and found that the bathroom inside was equipped with a shower, without a bathtub.

"Yes, what's the matter!" Leng Na said in the bedroom, "Come in, what's so beautiful in the hallway?"

I know I am sitting in the bed where Feng Qing used to sleep, with infinite emotions in my heart. Why was the same place once as terrifying as a battlefield, but today it is so approachable. And Leng Na is now ready to move down the mountain.

"This is Shilin's address and phone number. If you need anything, you can call me." Leng Na handed me a note and then said, "My things are not ready yet. I don't want to move at the moment."

"Where's Xia Huan?"

"She moved down the mountain first."

"When will you be ready? If you need my help, let me know."

"I don't know yet."

The next day, Leng Na told me, "I don't want to move down the mountain anymore. I want to move next to the school."

"Didn't you make an appointment with Xia Huan to go down the mountain and live together?"

"Senior, you don't know the real situation." Leng Na seemed to be full of grievances and said, "There are many things that I can't bear with Sister Xia Huan. For example, every morning when she wakes up, she sits at the bedside for a long time; that expression seems like I owe her hundreds of thousands; and then she kicks things under the bed with her feet, and I can't stand her attitude."

"I can't tell at all why she's so difficult to get along with! Alright, if you don't move down the mountain, maybe you'll have a better time."

Quickly, Leng Na rented a room on the second floor next to the school; I don't know how she did it because she didn't notify me to help move things.

Chapter 19   Beautiful photo

In the publishing department, I casually told my junior students:

"My family informed me to go back on the weekend."

"Is it going home for a blind date?" Leng Na sat nearby, probably the most concerned about this question!

I am only focused on work and unwilling to answer; A seemingly hopeless expression.

The next morning, when I was checking in for work, only three or four people came to the office, busy turning on the lights and doors and windows. Leng Na asked me to walk over and say:

"Senior, I want to show you something."

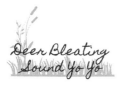

"Is it a new basketball? I said, if you want to play, you can continue to borrow it."

"No," Leng Na immediately took out the photo from her bag, handed it to me, and asked, "Isn't it very beautiful?"

"......" I took the photo and was dumbfounded, it turned out to be a photo of Feng Qing. She lay on the ground, showing a sweet smile. I just felt like I couldn't close my eyes immediately, but I couldn't open my mouth either. I was stunned.

"I'll leave it with you or give it to you."

I saw some words written at the back of the photo and didn't think it was suitable to accept it because she wrote:

"Leng Na, thank you for your love and care during this period. I will miss you, little elder sister."

Feng Qing presents

January 27th, 1983

Then I hesitated a bit and said, "How can I? This is not for me."

"It's okay, take it!" Leng Na smiled happily.

I always feel that Leng Na's long-term strange behavior must have a special reason, but I don't know what that means, I'm just willing to use patience to verify. Many things can be revealed or developed into results due to long enough time; Regardless of the outcome in the future, at this moment, I will try to respond with a calm and steady attitude; Moreover, I am a person who has practiced Tai Chi "Pushing Hands". Today, Leng Na took the initiative to send out photos, which was very sudden and the intention was also very obvious. At this moment, I would rather believe that Feng Qing agrees with her to do so, or that Leng Na really has sincerity or confidence to facilitate this good thing between me and Feng Qing.

At noon that day, I took the train south and sat in the last seat. The carriage shook uncontrollably, just like my mood at the moment. I got off at Tianzhong Station and in order to buy time, I called a taxi and it took me ten minutes to get home.

My parents went to the cabinet to find a pair of presbyopia glasses and took turns wearing them to look at the photos. My mother smiled and said:

"Ask her if she wants to come and play at our house."

"Mom, it's not the right time yet. I didn't invite her."

"So big, why is she still lying on the ground?" My father wore presbyopia glasses and carefully looked at it again and again.

"Modern young people are like this!"

"It's really beautiful, there's nothing wrong." After a while, my father said coldly, "You should focus on writing your paper, everything depends on fate; those who have it will be together."

My younger sister and I will first go to the backyard to see the flowers and the kitten, and then plan to stroll around the orchard outside the front wall; Before we could reach the orchard ahead, the kitten had already run over first. It would hide by the roadside, treating its owner's footsteps as moving prey, and suddenly jump out and embrace its owner's feet; Sometimes it can cause my younger sister to suddenly be frightened and scream. Planting a variety of crops in the orchard: longan, lychee, pineapple, papaya, tea tree, loquat, peach, banana, guavas, lemons, and cinnamon trees; Although they are not ornamental crops, they can also form a verdant landscape. We discovered the currently available fruits while browsing; It wasn't until our feet had enough exercise that we walked back, and the kitten was still leading the way.

Several sisters came back to their parents' house. I lay on the bed and listened to music. At the same time, I listened to the second sister and the fourth sister chatting. My second sister said, "I heard that Xiaoxia and his wife are getting divorced recently."

"Yes, he's really bad. He changed after less than a year of marriage. During his wife's pregnancy, he openly took young lady home to spend the night. When his wife gave birth, he asked for leave from the company and went on a date instead of taking care of his wife."

"His wife is really pitiful! But men are like this, they like to flirt outside. Your brother-in-law said, 'Men who are not flirtatious are great fools.' It's really infuriating to hear that."

"It's rare for men to behave like our father."

I listened and didn't bother to talk, because they were scolding men, and I was one of them. And I don't have any similar shortcomings for them to scold. Anyway, the things about the men they scold have nothing to do with me. I thought to myself, "You don't know that your younger brother is different from ordinary men, and I don't think I'm a big fool."

The next day, returning to school, it was already dusk. I found Leng Na still playing basketball. Based on usual habits, hasn't she been playing for two hours? I feel guilty, quickly run to the court to play a few games with her, and then invite her to dinner. After dinner, we sat on the grass in the US military residential area.

"My family has seen Feng Qing's photo; they didn't say anything and it was really beautiful. But they didn't encourage me, maybe they were afraid that if I failed, I would be very hurt."

At this moment, a dog gradually approached, and Leng Na smiled and said to the dog:

"Come here, your brother is here."

Because she knew that my zodiac sign belonged to dog, but I still didn't agree. I said, "How can you say that?" Then I turned to the dog and said, "Come here, you should call me Uncle."

"Hahaha -" Leng Na smiled and bent over.

"I once went to Tamkang to find my classmates. That was at night when I walked into the black alley and saw a big dog running towards me, barking fiercely. At first, I was a bit flustered."

"What happened later?"

"Throwing some biscuit on the ground, the dog put in a lot of effort, but still couldn't bite; I took the opportunity and retreated all over."

"Well, that's a great method."

"Can you have a frank and unreserved conversation with Feng Qing?"

"Of course." Leng Na nodded in affirmation and then said, "If you want to write to her, it's best to let me know first, so she doesn't say what happened to me."

"I want to focus on reading and no longer write letters."

"It's also good."

"Can you ask her by the way if she would like to meet with me?"

"I'll make the call, you follow; if she wants, you can talk, okay?"

"It's better to have a face-to-face interview! It's inappropriate to talk on the phone." I sat still and said, "I once asked her on the phone: 'Why did you

suddenly move up the mountain in the first place?' Feng Qing said: 'Can't I move up the mountain? I'm just doing my homework, but you're telling people this everywhere?' I asked again: 'Then, when I came to find you after you arriving at Shanzai Hou, why did you open the door and smile?' Feng Qing said, 'I feel very sad talking to you; please, don't, call, again,' then hang up the phone with just one sound."

Leng Na smiled and said, "I can imagine the way she spoke at that time."

After a moment of contemplation, Leng Na solemnly said, "Let me give it a try and become a matchmaker, okay?"

"Thank you."

"However, I can't guarantee success, I'm just willing to give it a try," Leng Na tilted her head and said, "Are you feeling any better now?"

At night, both my Korean roommate and I were preparing for the exam, but I couldn't help but pick up the photo and stare blankly. My roommate said, "Whose photo are you looking at?"

"That's from the dance department. It's important for you to take the exam, don't be as distracted as I am. My self-control seems to be insufficient."

"Exam? What are you afraid of? Didn't you hear someone say, 'Good sanitary pads don't need to be thick'? Let me take a look at the photo."

I handed it to him and he said, "Hmm! It's like a movie star." At this moment, Leng Na came to me downstairs and reminded me:

"Senior, you can't write letters or make phone calls anymore. Otherwise, Feng Qing will say you have no backbone. If you mess things up, I don't care about you."

"No, I just want to read."

"You! I've seen through it; you'll definitely go find her again."

"Really not, the matter is not yet settled. Please don't say it out, okay?"

Chapter 20 To Annoy the Benefactor

A week has passed since I received the photo, and I believe Leng Na will also be busy with my affairs at this time.

In the evening, I met Leng Na and asked, "Have you contacted Feng Qing recently?"

"I'll help you make the phone call, let's go."

"I have no intention of talking to her on the phone," I hesitated and said, "Don't let her know I'm standing next to you."

"Okay."

Leng Na called Taoyuan and Feng Qing answered the phone. I could only hear Leng Na's voice, and she said:

"Feng Qing, how has the situation been lately?"

"……"

"Oh, oh, that's it."

"……"

"Help? I think both of you need help! He's, my senior."

"……"

"His personality is like this; how come you don't know."

"……"

"That's right! Just like taking care of my sister, as long as you can get happiness, I certainly respect your choices."

"……"

"Feng Qing, can my senior talk to you?"

"……"

"Okay, let's talk about it after school starts!" Leng Na hung up the receiver and turned to me, saying, "Feng Qing said, 'He's not giving up yet? Let's talk about it after school starts!'"After taking a few steps, she said, "She said she has a boyfriend and is very stable. He's staying at her home now."

"I don't compete with others," I said angrily, with a very firm attitude.

Walking to the side of the court, Leng Na said:

"You go first, I want to be quiet here."

"Why did you use to help me with this before? I'm not a spineless person; why didn't you get to know me first and act rashly?"

"Senior, I just want to help you," Leng Na sat on the stairs with a painful expression.

"Come to my place, I'll return the photo to you."

Leng Na is standing downstairs in the dormitory, waiting for me to bring the photo. Taking back the photo, she said in frustration:

"Senior, study hard. I need to go back."

I entered the dormitory and scribbled a letter to Feng Qing, writing:

March 27th, 1983

Classmate Feng:

Leng Na called you, and I stood by to listen. I'm going to tell you something here, hoping to clear my name.

Previously, she often suggested several classmates to go to Tamsui to eat seafood. However, I refused because I was busy with my homework and worked in the publishing department. Occasionally, I had a few more conversations with other girls, and she might come over, intentionally or unintentionally interfering and "breaking up". For a long time, she has borrowed the ball from the literary institute from me. Every evening when I go out to eat, I always see her reading by the court with a basketball at her feet; I said hello and she just started pitching. Many classmates mocked her, and I became anxious for her. Until a few days ago, I had to mention your name and ask about your situation.

This evening, Leng Na said he wanted to ask Feng Qing for me, and I stood next to the phone. After hanging up the phone, she said, "Feng Qing said we should talk about it after school starts." I calmly said, "I won't compete with others." Walking to the side of the court, she asked me to go first, and she wanted to sit quietly. I said, "Why did you use to help me with this before? I'm not a spineless person; why didn't you get to know me first and act rashly?" She said sadly, "Senior, I just wanted to help you." She asked me to study hard and went back on her own.

She thinks she's nosy, but I feel unlucky. Of course, this has nothing to do with you.

Sign without intention

I feel like my soul is empty and I have finished delivering the letter to the post office. On the way back to the dormitory, on a dark downhill road, there was a girl squatting by the road, tying her shoelaces. I didn't notice anyone, but I kicked her over.

"Hey-yo! You're going to die."

"If die, forget it." It seems like I shouted louder than her.

The next morning, I carried my bag and prepared to go to the Academia Sinica to read. On the way to the bus stop, Leng Na was coming. She was going to work in the publishing department. I said seriously, "I sent a letter to Feng Qing in Taoyuan last night, and now I'm going to the Academia Sinica."

Leng Na's attitude was cold and silent, staying by the road without saying a word. I didn't say much and hurried away.

Reading at the Academia Sinica, about half past ten, two Korean students also came. We have lunch together and then rest at the nearby Hu Shi Park. One Korean said, "What kind of flower is this? It's so beautiful!" Another said, "Yellow oleander, be careful, it may be toxic." I looked uninterested. Next, the Koreans sang the songs they had recently learned:

> The grasslands of Qinghai are endless at a glance, with Himalayan peaks connected to the horizon. Ancient sages and wise people of the past built their homes here, standing for five thousand years amidst wind and rain. The Republic of China, the Republic of China, can withstand the test; As long as the water of the Yellow River continues, the Republic of China, the Republic of China, will continue for generations and forever.

"Why do you say that as long as the water in the Yellow River continues, the Republic of China will last forever? It seems that there is no such inevitability! Just like Mencius used 'water must flow downward' to prove that human nature must be kind-hearted. I can also say: 'Water must flow downward, so human nature must be evil.'" At this time, my heart seems much narrower.

"I have a friend who is a doctor and he told me that his medical skills are very skilled. He only needs to make a small incision for cecal surgery. Later, he found out that his wife had an affair, and the situation became very intense; He said that during that period, whenever he operated on someone in a fit of anger, the wound grew longer." Another Korean friend knew that I was in a bad mood recently and used these words to correct me. I sincerely thank him.

Leng Na appeared on the basketball court again after three days of silence. I walked side by side with another male senior from the literary institute, and I invited him to play ball together. The three of us finished playing ball, had dinner together, and after dinner, we went to buy fruits together. Walking downstairs to Leng Na's residence, she handed me the fruit and turned to the senior student behind her, saying:

"Senior, you can go back first. I need to go back and change clothes."

"Oh!" The senior seemed to have been mercilessly driven away, a bit embarrassed, but also helpless. He only said, "Then, I'll go first, goodbye!" And ran away without a trace.

Leng Na took the ball upstairs, changed his clothes, and came downstairs. We walked side by side, and within a few dozen steps, we encountered an intersection. Leng Na said to me:

"Senior, you go back first, I'll walk this way." After speaking, turn right and accelerate her steps.

"Where are you going?" I feel a bit puzzled.

"Take a walk." Leng Na didn't turn back and continued to move forward.

I followed closely behind, passing near the church, and I spoke:

"Feng Qing……"

"How is Feng Qing?" Leng Na suddenly let out a loud roar, with a strong temper.

With her mouth closed, she continued to move forward and finally stopped next to the Wenda Ornamental Column. I sat on the iron chair by the roadside, Leng Na didn't say a word, standing facing the Ornamental Column for a long time. I think she's really making trouble for no reason, so I stood up and said rudely:

"Go in now."

We had nothing to say along the way and walked back to the school. She said in a stern and sad tone:

"What are you doing writing a letter for? Those are tactful opening remarks, do you know? Do you know what others think?"

"Is that so? I'm sorry."

"......" Leng Na ignored me and quickly walked towards the US military dependents' area.

I don't want to explain or follow anymore, so I walked back to school alone.

For several days in a row, Leng Na ignored me. Until one day, while working in the publishing department, I said to her:

"You have always been enthusiastic about helping me, innocent people are originally innocent, no matter what others say about you. I will clarify the rumor for you."

"Every time I think of Yiti's malicious words, I feel very sad," she said, almost crying.

"Don't worry, you are innocent."

Chapter 21   Tired but futile

Since Leng Na stated that what she had discussed with Feng Qing on the phone a few days ago were just "tactful opening remarks," she must continue singing this play.

Without prior contact, my mother came to Chinese Culture University and said to me:

"Where is the girl from the dance department? Find her and let me see."

"Mom, I'm just about to rush to write my paper. Can I skip this matter for now?"

"Just take a look, it won't take up much of your time."

"Please sit in the dormitory, and I will go outside to inquire about the situation."

I went straight to the publishing department to find Leng Na and said:

"My mother came and said she wanted to see Feng Qing."

"No, no. How could Feng Qing agree? If your mother wants to talk to someone so formally, Feng Qing will definitely be frightened."

"What should I do? "

"You told her that Feng Qing has no classes today and is not in school."

My mother was very disappointed and I sent her to Taipei Station. At the West Highway Station, I held her handbag and said:

"Mom, please rest assured that if she is not a good girl, I will definitely not want her. Please rest assured. I didn't mean to make you sad, this matter is really difficult to handle."

"You need to keep your eyes open."

"I know." I watched her get on the bus and take her seat before I left the station.

Many of my relatives, or young people from the same village who are the same age as me or younger than me, have posted news about getting married, and my mother had to attend their weddings. During the wedding ceremony, which was adorned with beautiful clothes, vibrant demeanor, and noisy voices and laughter, others would always ask, "Has Wang Wang found a partner? It's time to get married."

"He is busy writing his paper and hasn't reached a consensus yet." My mother repeatedly dragged this kind of melancholy home.

On the weekend, I went back to Nantou, and my family members all had objections to Feng Qing.

"Brother, I think you are trapped in a fog, and we are all bystanders. Nothing is this outrageous anymore, you are too stubborn."

"It was Leng Na who said he wanted to help and kept me from giving up or leaving."

"Leng Na, Leng Na. Leave it all to Leng Na, so who does Feng Qing mean? If she is interested in you, she will take the initiative to seize the opportunity. How can there be any reason to avoid it from beginning to end? Can you still say that she is interested in you?"

"That's right! That's right! I'm very stupid, but I tell you, since there are boys like me in the world, I believe there must be girls like me. I'm just looking for someone like me."

The next morning, my mother was organizing her household chores in the kitchen and calmly said to my father:

"The girl in Taoyuan was very strange from the beginning. I didn't appreciate her, but Wang Wang insisted on this one."

"I don't care about him anymore. Even if you persuade him, he won't listen." said my father, putting on his hat and walking out the front door.

"Mom," I walked into the kitchen from behind the house and said with sadness, "I think she's better than others, and she's also willing to socialize with me. Otherwise, why should I be obsessed with her? You say you no longer like this unmarried young lady; how will you get along with her in the future?"

"......" My mother was too lazy to answer.

In the evening, I arrived at the house of the third elder sister of Yonghe, and the third elder sister said:

"Our family once called me and they were very disappointed with you, saying that our parents have loved you since childhood, which was in vain; Now that you have grown up, you are unwilling to listen to their advice."

I silently bear the pressure from all parties, and it's useless to talk too much anyway. Returning to school and meeting Leng Na, she said:

"I saw Feng Qing and she asked me to ignore you. Her mother said that if you greet her in the future, she will only need to respond with a salute; if you don't greet her, it's okay."

"Since Feng Qing already has a boyfriend, the last time you said she promised to have a meeting with me after school started, it was really unnecessary."

"Is your definition of a friend so narrow?" Leng Na sternly scolded, "She already has a boyfriend and lives at her house. She's willing to talk to you and be an ordinary friend, can't she?"

"......" I reflected quietly for a moment and said with certainty, "It's my fault. Okay, anyway, I'm willing to talk to her. Please tell her."

"Hmm! I'll give it a try and ask her out to meet."

"Thank you."

Two days later, Leng Na visited me with a gloomy expression.

"What's wrong with you? You look unhappy."

"How could it not be for Feng Qing."

"What happened?"

"I've failed." Leng Na almost cried out and said, "What did I owe you in my previous life? I've always been angry about your things in this life."

"I'm really sorry, please don't worry about these things in the future."

"Feng Qing said today that she is only willing to greet you on the way, not to keep an appointment. She is very determined."

"Feng Qing's attitude has always been so inexplicable, and I have seen it many times. You don't need to worry about this matter anymore, let's call it a day. I'm sorry to have kept you running around for so long, but I still appreciate you very much."

Since the matter has come to an end, I think the top priority is to refute the rumor for Leng Na. I should not walk with her to avoid classmates mocking her. At noon, I walked out of the publishing department and said to Leng Na that I would eat on my own from now on, so I accelerated my pace and prepared to leave. Leng Na smiled and said:

"It's okay! Let's eat out together."

"I really want to eat inside," I quickly left.

In the evening, after taking a shower, I took a nap and woke up around 8 o'clock. My Korean roommate walked up to the bed and asked me, "Leng Na is playing basketball on the field, why didn't you go?"

"Do you see her playing ball? I don't want to play anymore." I feel like I can settle down and read without paying attention to that troublesome matter.

From a few years ago to the present, many women, especially younger students, have really had feelings for me. For example, someone said, "My sister-in-law urged me to get married quickly, saying that if I saw an honest person, I would get married as soon as possible." Someone handed me something, but intentionally or unintentionally stretched it too far and shook my hand, as if to test my reaction. Someone gave me a small card with stars and big footprints painted on it, as if it meant a date or something. Some puns are used: "Senior, when will you help me 'hug' (referring to helping her bring books)?" Some people used the "borrowing but not returning" method, perhaps to create opportunities for conversation; If it's not an important book that I have to ask for, I often don't ask for it from now on, just give it to her. Someone emphasized to me, "I will definitely be obedient."

Someone took advantage of me going down the mountain, bought flowers, ran to my dormitory, and in front of my roommate, inserted the flowers into my large cup. A married female classmate came to school with a child in her arms. In front of me, she openly asked everyone, "Do you see if he looks like Wang Wang?" "Busy is blind, busy cannot be used as an excuse." Someone wrote a New Year card and at the end wrote, "Wishing you a happy

New Year and tender mountains and rivers." Two women I know were chatting, and as I walked by, I overheard one saying, "Since ancient times, no great man has been monopolized by one woman." The other succinctly and forcefully said, "That's right!" I treat those comments as wind that has blown in my ears and don't take them to heart. I don't need to make any serious statements either, because I don't have any ulterior motives or behavior towards girls. This may be my way of accepting my father's style.

This steadfast attitude can also be attributed to a certain student sister who told me in my sophomore year: "If any girl is interested in you, if you don't want to develop further with her, you don't have to say anything, just pretend you don't know. Because human emotions are short-lived, time can solve such problems for you; explaining them is not good."

I don't often work in the publishing department anymore because I'm busy writing my master's thesis; Leng Na is in a bad mood and often lies on the table. A few days later, it turned into a leave of absence and not coming to work. Sometimes, it is said that she is particularly enthusiastic. While working in the publishing department, she meets people and asks, "Where is Senior Wang Wang going? Does he go to the Academia Sinica?" Some people think she really has an urgent matter and come to inform me at night. I have always been puzzled by the series of strange movements made by Leng Na.

Chapter 22   Family Emotions Near Collapse

My younger sister couldn't help but write to Feng Qing, wanting to know her true situation.

Miss Feng:

I am Wang Wang's younger sister, perhaps one year older than you, and currently teaching in primary school.

Our family has always been extremely concerned about my brother's friendship. From his description, we believe that you are a dignified and virtuous good girl, and my parents are happy to accept this news.

Why has this matter been delayed so long? Is your conversation a bit vague, making my brother feel confused? Or is it purely a misunderstanding by my brother?

In terms of relationships, due to my brother's non-casual and insistent attitude, he is still at a loss to this day. His character is good, and his emotions are also very focused. He has been repeatedly hit by you, and we all feel that he has suffered a lot.

Obviously, the number of times he goes home has decreased, and he no longer calls home on time. Every time he comes back, his sad and gloomy expression makes us see it in our eyes and feel pain in our hearts. He had an argument with my family and said, "Since there are boys like me in the world, I believe there are also girls like me." We were at a loss.

For others and for yourself, please cooperate with us and give me a definite answer, so that we can handle things easily. Thank you!

Sincerely,

○ ○ ○

Meanwhile, my younger sister told me over the phone that she had already written to Feng Qing, asking me to be willing to accept any outcome.

Leng Na met me on campus and said, "It looks like you have something to say to me."

"No."

"Liar! Speak quickly."

"Well, let me think about it." I thought for a few seconds and said, "Okay, I'll say it. You once told me before: 'As long as you appreciate it, pursue it elsewhere.' I am willing to accept this suggestion. My family members were very happy when they saw that I finally figured it out. Seeing them happy made me happy too."

Leng Na laughed and for a moment, he tightened his clothes and said, "The wind is so strong."

"My younger sister called and said she wrote to Feng Qing."

"Just give it a try, Feng Qing will definitely be scared."

"She used to never reply to me, I don't know if she will reply to my younger sister."

"I will persuade her to reply to the letter."

"Thank you."

Quickly, my younger sister received a reply and immediately called me to inform me, "Brother, Feng Qing replied and said she already has a boyfriend. You don't have to be sad, there are still many opportunities."

"……" I couldn't answer for a moment. After standing for a few seconds, I said, "Please send me her reply for me to see."

I received the letter and at night, I showed it to Leng Na. She stood under the streetlight reading the letter.

"Last time you said you wanted to persuade Feng Qing to reply, she replied to such a letter."

"Just believe in her."

"Leng Na, Feng Qing is very kind to me. Her tone has become gentle, she wants it. Look at what she wrote."

"Alright, Alright," Leng Na felt impatient and didn't want to listen anymore. She scolded, "I see you don't even have the mood to write your paper. Is that okay?"

"This is just my guess, I don't know if it's right. However, her attitude seems to have improved."

"May I bring her to see you?"

"Can she trust you? Does she listen to your words?"

"Of course, I believe it! I was so kind to her and always took care of her."

"Okay, when will it be?"

"This requires waiting for the appropriate moment." she said more calmly. "Last time I saw Feng Qing, I said, 'My senior is very nice!' She didn't say anything, just smiled."

"No matter what, let her come forward and make it clear."

"I want you to have beautiful memories in the future, and I will hand you over to Feng Qing for safekeeping."

I finally heard the clearest promise, and a thousand thanks are in my heart. I think I must persist until the end.

Shortly after, my mother called to ask me to go home. I had just stepped into the house and it was already over five o'clock in the afternoon.

"Where did parents go?"

"Go to the fields," said my younger sister, "Feng Qing's matter really should come to an end."

"Oh, what do you understand? Leng Na told me very clearly, just wait for a while."

"Someone else's dog came and killed our big cock; Mom has been depressed these days, worrying about this and that."

"……" I only took off one of my leather shoes and didn't take them off anymore. I lay on the chair with a blank expression.

"Our second sister knows that you are coming back, and she will come back after get off work."

At seven o'clock in the evening, our whole family sat around for dinner. Before we could finish a mouthful of food, the conversation had already begun. My mother said:

"Since the girl in Taoyuan replied that she already has a boyfriend, let's look for another one. We're not afraid we won't find a good girl."

"Mom, she's really kind to me. Leng Na definitely said she wants to help me."

"If she really intends to socialize with you, I think she is arrogant and wants to overwhelm our family, right?"My younger sister really got angry and said, "That kind of girl doesn't match our family. "

"She's not, what do you know?"

"Who doesn't understand her? Because she's beautiful, you ignore others' opinions and say she's all right."

"I'll tell you, she's interested in me, so I'll wait until today. Otherwise, why should I? You shouldn't have said such things."

"Don't be too stubborn," said the second sister. "I think there's a problem with this one. Let's find another one. There are many young ladies outside."

"No, no; when I say no, it means no."

"Humph!" the younger sister also shouted, "He has such a temper, persuasion is useless."

"Wang Wang!" Mother once again urged, "We are for your own good and we are worried that you will be deceived."

"Should you be so disobedient? You keep saying she's interested in you, and our parents want you to take her home to show us, but where is she?"

"The most useless thing! You are so self-righteous." My younger sister became more and more ruthless as she spoke.

"You should accept our advice."

"Ah! - I won't listen. She's very kind to me. You insist on taking us apart, Go to hell!" I interrupted my second sister, blushing and standing up to charge out, forcefully pushing open the screen door. With a "ram" the screen door almost fell off.

In an instant, there was silence inside and outside. I stood behind the house, leaning on the pillar. My mother came out, took my hand, and said softly:

"Come in and eat, it's all up to you to decide," After speaking, she led me back to my seat.

"I don't care, you can take whoever you want." Father blushed, panicked and sad, said: "Anyway, I have prepared the gift money. If you say you want to get married, whoever she is, it's up to you. When the time comes, I will just hand over the gift money to you."

"We won't stop you, don't worry," said my second sister, "Hurry up and have a meal."

The next day, I returned to campus and just passed under a street lamp. In the pitch black, someone reached out to intercept me. Upon closer inspection, she was Leng Na.

"Let's go, senior. Please have some food."

"No need."

"Let's go, I'll treat you."

"I have been transferred back home again; I am afraid to go home now, and I am also afraid to make phone calls because of Feng Qing's situation, and I have no way to explain it." I started walking with her and walked towards the store area.

"Previously, when you called Feng Qing, she didn't even listen, so she put the receiver on the table. After a long time, she picked it up and listened, only to find that you were still talking endlessly."

"Joke. They put the receiver on the table, how could I not know? They're exaggerating."

"I used to talk to Xiao Mei before, and she said why chasing girls is so painful; all the classmates in their class are laughing at you, like a big fool."

We bought fruit, but Leng Na refused to let me pay, and then we walked to the US military area.

"Senior, a while ago, Feng Qing was busy attending a program in the TV University City. Do you know?"

"Oh, is there such a thing?" I said, "The entertainment industry is a whirlpool, and people who get involved are often no longer as simple as those outside. They say, 'Spring water is clear in the mountains, and once it comes out of the mountains, it easily turns into turbid water.' There are very few people in the entertainment industry who are emotionally stable, and there are relatively few who stay together for a lifetime. This is the reason why I despise them."

"Feng Qing said that in the future, if her husband wants to interfere with her personal development in expertise, she will not allow it."

"Dance is an art, but why speak so strongly? If she appeared on TV not for the sake of art, but for her vanity, I would also look down on her." I continued, "The good girl in my mind is a person with all three aspects: wisdom, beauty, and moral integrity. Nowadays, most of the movie stars are incomplete."

Returning to the downstairs of Leng Na's residence, she said, "Come and take a look. This dog is just as foolish as you."

I thought she was making trouble for no reason, so I ignored her.

She quickly went upstairs and came down with a bottle of premium honey, insisting that I take it. I had to accept the gift, but I looked disappointed and said:

"A few days ago, Chen Tai laughed at me and said he thought it was strange. Wang Ya, Doudou, and Xiao Ru were all so kind to me, while I chose the one from the dance department. He said, Xiao Ru is stronger than Feng Qing in all aspects."

"Don't listen to Chen Tai's nonsense, how can Xiao Ru compare to Feng Qing."

"I'm just saying it, I didn't mean to pursue Xiao Ru. Li Pu lives in the dormitory next to me, and he really wants to chase Xiao Ru, but does Xiao Ru like him? That's not necessarily the case."

Chapter 23　Gradually Becoming Clear

I waited and waited, but couldn't get any good news, so I wrote another letter to ask Feng Qing.

Feng Qing:

On the road in Huagang, Leng Na pointed at the dog by the roadside and said to me, "Look, it's silly, just like you." I remember she mocked me more than once. I didn't ask why; I just hope you can tell me what's going on.

Leng Na is very pitiful. I don't know why she is particularly eager to help me with making friends; However, whenever the attempt failed, she was so sad that she almost cried. I kept saying, "I'm really sorry, don't work anymore." She asked me, "What did I owe you in my previous life? I've always been angry about your affairs in this life!"

I know you are a good girl, but you once disregarded my foolish vows. Think about it! How broad is the definition of 'interpersonal relationship'; If the personalities of two people match, they will have a deep friendship, and if they don't match, let it fade. Why be overly afraid? Am I really as terrifying as a raging beast? How dare you do things without leaving a way out?

In the future, we may have a foothold in society, and there may always be times when we meet. Please do not block all the paths ahead.

This Thursday at 12 noon, I will be waiting for you at the door of Liangyou Hall. Please accept my invitation and come to the appointment.

Sincerely,
Wang Wang

On Thursday noon, Feng Qing did not attend the appointment. On Saturday afternoon, I called Gongguan and her elder male cousin answered with a gentle tone, saying, "She's back in Taoyuan, not here." This was her elder male cousin's best attitude ever.

I immediately called Taoyuan and Feng Qing answered the phone.

"Who are you?"

"I am Wang Wang."

"……" She didn't say a word and gently hung it up.

A few nights later, I told Leng Na, "The day before yesterday, I arranged to meet Feng Qing, but she didn't come to the appointment."

"You deserve it!" Leng Na was a little unhappy and said, "Who wants you to go find her? This way just give you a taste of what it's like to wait for someone else and teach you a lesson."

"This afternoon, I called her, but she didn't speak."

"Feng Qing asked me to ignore you."

"No, no, she lied to you." Because I felt that Feng Qing's attitude had changed for the better, I felt more confident; at this time, my tone was like coquettishness.

Leng Na smiled, and I followed suit with a silly smile; Suddenly, she tightened her face and said, "Serious." Her expression became very strange, as if she was crying and laughing at the same time. After a while, she asked me:

"Are you going to call her again in the future?"

"No, no."

"Humph! I don't know how many times you have declared it." Leng Na snapped, looking elsewhere, and then said, "Didn't you say that someone else wants to introduce you to someone? Why did you call Feng Qing again?"

"Actually, I'm worried that if Feng Qing wants me, what should I do if I make a mistake? I don't want to disappoint her."

"That's right! That's right! You're all right," Leng Na said with a disdainful expression. Quickly, she said, "There is a clothing store in Taipei with a great sale for export. Do you want to go shopping?"

"......" I didn't show any interest and said, "When she moved up the mountain before, you didn't encourage me to chase her shamelessly, otherwise I would have chased her long ago."

"Go after it! Go after it."

"......"I am speechless.

"It's worth it, this price. People always cherish things that are not easy to get."

"Leng Na, your heart is too hard. Their attitude is very soft, can't you feel it?" I complained softly.

"It seems like it's all my responsibility."

"Sorry! I often get so impatient that things go wrong; This is my fault."

Later, several times, Leng Na discovered that I and Xiao Ru were happily chatting by the roadside. Leng Na wrote a letter to me:

Dear senior:

I will do my best to help you with Feng Qing's matter; whether it succeeds or not depends on your luck. You don't have to thank me either. I don't ask for any thanks; But it's still the old saying: "Please don't 'sorry' Li Pu." (I believe you understand what I mean) Otherwise, our friendship over the past year may also deteriorate. My words are all serious. Don't forget, Li Pu is also my respected senior, and I don't want to see him suffer. If you do something wrong to him, it means you have also offended me. I believe you understand. This is not a threat, it's just my wish; I hope you don't disappoint me. Both of you are my good seniors. I hope it will always be.

Sincerely,

Leng Na

Leng Na wrote this letter asking me not to pursue Xiao Ru, otherwise it would be an offense to Li Pu; To offend Li Pu is to offend her. But as far as I know, Xiao Ru is not very interested in Li Pu, and Li Pu has not explicitly stated his pursuit. At most, it is just a secret love in his heart! Why does Leng Na restrict my dating partners? She emphasized that it was to be loyal to Li Pu, did the depth of love and righteousness really reach this level? I have accumulated countless doubts in my heart and have to write to Feng Qing again, writing:

Dear Feng Qing:

Have you ever thought about it? If you have a stable mood, the efficiency of reading can be improved several times. People should have been honest with each other. I am willing to have a written conversation with you without any hesitation. If there is anything presumptuous, please do not take it amiss.

During this summer vacation, Leng Na came out every evening to play basketball, which cost a lot of time and money; Finally, it moved and softened my heart, so I took the initiative to ask about you, and she was very happy. A few days later, she brought your jade photo. In an instant, I was confused. She said, "Here you are." I couldn't suppress my excitement and ran home that afternoon; Leng Na smiled happily. Unexpectedly, a few days later, she took me to the phone to listen, and the content of your conversation surprised and disappointed me, so I immediately returned your jade photo to her; She couldn't speak and was heartbroken for a long time, planning to stop talking to me from then on. She said, "What are you doing writing a letter for? Those are tactful opening remarks, do you know? Do you know what others think?

She always says that you already have a boyfriend, but for a long time, she has said intermittently: "Senior, it's worth it! This price." "People often cherish things that are not easy to get." "Let you have beautiful memories in the future." "I will hand you over to Feng Qing for safekeeping." These words have kept me in a state of confusion.

It's too strange. How much does she know about you? How much do you know about her? From her conversation, I believe you are willing to greet me politely on the way. However, since I deeply felt that she was well intentioned, in order to fulfill her wish, I let her try.

Perhaps your composure is so extraordinary, in short, it has been too long. Who dares to believe that we will be together? If you are willing to give me a kind face, please let Leng Na know.

PS.

1. Please don't let Leng Na know that I am writing this letter to avoid making her angry.

2. I have already felt exhausted about this matter. If you don't respond, then there won't be a chance in the future. Do you think it's reasonable?

Sincerely,
Wang Wang

Since the letter has been sent, I believe Feng Qing will respond accordingly. Therefore, I tried to visit Leng Na. We stood in the middle of the stairs from the first floor to the second floor, about five steps apart. I leaned against the wall and asked:

"Have you heard from Feng Qing?"

"I called her again for you." Leng Na said angrily, "She said a lot of bad things that are hard to hear. I don't want to tell you."

"Alright, don't mention it anymore." I got angry and quickly went downstairs to leave. Upon seeing this scene, Leng Na must have thought that I completely hated Feng Qing from then on.

Li Pu was Leng Na's exclusive senior in college, and now he occasionally visits Leng Na's residence. One day, he found out that Leng Na had once visited the Xingtian Palace to pay respects and draw lots. The divine sign was placed on her desk, which was a lucky sign with the following content:

> Su Qin's outstanding eloquence was enough to make a living out of society.
> The opportunity for wealth and fame lies in this performance.
> We Should be well-cultivated and pay attention to Yin De and virtue.
> A bright future and a prosperous career can be expected.

Li Pu is also my good friend and has heard a lot about Feng Qing's affairs. He found that the auspicious sign placed on Leng Na's table strengthened her confidence and intended to follow Su Qin's eloquent words to achieve her aspirations. However, there is an annotation on this divine sign itself, which reads: "I'm afraid there may be a lack of Yin virtue, which may hinder the great opportunity." Li Pu returned to the Dazhuangguan dormitory and kindly came to tell me about this. I said in confusion, "Duke Guan advised her to cultivate Yin virtue? I'll pay attention next time. It's true that I saw "*Golden Plum in the Vase*" on her desk a few days ago."

One evening, when I met Leng Na on my way, she enthusiastically said, "Senior, you're so busy writing your paper. If you need my help copying it, I can help. "

"It's not yet the time for finalization. If you're willing to help, there's some urgent information to check the page numbers. Let's check together, okay?"

"Okay, bring the data to my dormitory tonight, let's check together!"

"Um! I think it can be completed in three nights at most."

I returned to my dormitory and came to Leng Na with five or six thick books. After dinner, I immediately started working. I passed by the room next to Leng Na's and took a look, only to find that there was no one inside; I asked Leng Na:

"Is the classmate next door sleeping on the floor? Why not sleep on the bed?"

"There is a man and a woman living inside, both of whom are in their junior year."

"Oh, cohabitation?"

"Outside the school, there are many classmates living together. During school, they lived together, but after graduation, they went their separate ways and were unrelated to each other."

At eleven o'clock in the evening, I temporarily left the information here in Leng Na and returned to the dormitory empty handed to sleep.

The next day, after dinner, I bought some fruits to give Leng Na, and then started checking the information. Leng Na took out two keys and gave them to me, saying:

"If you come to our place, you must trouble someone else to come out and open the gate. It's very inconvenient. One of these two is for the gate and the other is for this room; here you are."

"Okay!" I took the key and put it in my pocket.

Around ten o'clock, someone knocked at the door and Leng Na stood up to open it; It turned out that several colleagues from the publishing department were visiting, but they stood by the bedroom door and refused to come in; I turned around and saw that they smiled slightly and immediately left. I said to Leng Na:

"What are they doing? Their faces look strange."

"They dare not come in, probably because they saw you here."

"Tell them clearly so that they don't make a fuss."

After checking the information for a while, Leng Na said:

"This afternoon, the mother of the girl next door came here."

"Isn't she angry when she sees her daughter living with a boy?"

"No way! Her mother is very happy, saying that the trend of the times is already like this, just follow the free will of young people."

"Humph! There's such a mother."

On the third night, I came to Leng Na again.

Around 9:30, Leng Na turned on the recorder and listened to popular Western music; The rhythm is too turbulent, and my whole heart cannot calm down, almost unable to sit still. That night, the perfume in the bedroom was very strong. Leng Na combed her hair with a comb, and the smell came in bursts. I realized that the situation was not right and said in a probing tone:

"Leng Na, I don't know if you have contacted Feng Qing? How is her attitude?"

"Feng Qing?...... You still mention her?" Leng Na's voice trembled like an electric shock, and her face almost turned black. She started running and rushed downstairs.

I calmly went downstairs and searched outside, but couldn't see any sign of her, so I had to go upstairs and sit in place waiting. My eyes were looking around the room, and I saw the "*Golden Plum in the Vase*" and the "Divine Sign for Cultivating Yin Virtue" on the desk.

About ten minutes later, Leng Na returned to the dormitory and sat on the bed. She bent her knees, lowered her head, put her face against her knees, and spread her hair; her hands were placed around her head and knees, with her palms in the air.

Unexpectedly, tonight I finally confirmed the crux of the Feng Qing incident.

Since getting to know Feng Qing, I have given her countless calls, nervously reminding and correcting her, both right and wrong; When awake, it is Feng Qing, and when sleeping, it is also Feng Qing; Worry is Feng Qing, and thought is also Feng Qing; She already holds an unshakable position in my heart; Even, I am willing to sacrifice my life as long as she says to me personally that she truly loves me.

At this moment, I suddenly woke up. When Feng Qing first met Leng Na, she made a mistake and lost the whole game. Feng Qing didn't know that Leng Na was an enemy she hadn't noticed. She just wanted to be friends with her and have a good heart to heart relationship, so in a game of pretending to be dead, Leng Na secretly stabbed Feng Qing fiercely. No, it was probably a soft knife cut that didn't make her consciously die.

During the days when Feng Qing moved to live on the mountain, Leng Na's most crucial measure was to do everything possible to prevent Feng Qing and I from having the opportunity to meet and talk alone; Coincidentally, Feng Qing let it out on her own, saying that she and I don't see each other, are in a state of no contact or communication, which allows Leng Na to do whatever she wants. Therefore, she played and cut and killed us recklessly. Leng Na began to fabricate rumors and destroy my image. At the critical moment when I was facing the most danger, she deceived me with lies and encouraged me to strive to jump into the abyss. In just a few days, it was enough for Feng Qing to flee in a panic and move back to the Gongguan, feeling frightened and regretful; Perhaps Leng Na also provided some thoughtful suggestions so that she can safely protect herself from my harm in the future. When Feng Qing expressed gratitude, Leng Na asked for a photo of Feng Qing; And that photo was later used by Leng Na to deal with me.

I sat in the chair, pondering in despair for a moment, and then calmly said:

"Leng Na, you made it clear a long time ago that you wanted to help facilitate the matter between me and Feng Qing. I have always trusted you very much. You have spent a lot of time and money, and I am very clear that I plan to repay you in the future. Although I did not say it, I have already had an idea in my heart. As long as you help successfully, I will give you a very generous reward." I couldn't continue, shook my head silently, took out the key from my pocket, placed it on the table, and said, "I'll give you the key back." After finishing, I picked up the books and turned to leave.

I gently closed the door, but Leng Na didn't move.

It's the end of 1983 now, my goodness! I am a silly bird of paradise. For a year now, I have been striving to dance the "dance of choosing a mate", but what about the female bird I am pursuing? But there was not even a shadow; I don't know what I'm fussing about?

Stepping out of the building, I called Taoyuan and Feng Qing's mother answered the phone, calling Feng Qing to come and listen.

"Hello, this is Wang Wang."

"Wang Wang, I tell you, Leng Na is interested in you. She's not helping you."

"Yes, I have received the evidence." After a pause, I said: "Would you like to meet me?"

"I really have a boyfriend now, I don't think it's necessary to meet again."

"Sorry, I don't have any copper coins left. That's all I can say. Goodbye."

Leng Na took sick leave from then on and did not work in the publishing department for a long time.

A Nightmare - Heaven's Envy

The mountains and hills are high and low, with lush vegetation,
The clumps of bamboo made the path a maze.
In the silence, suddenly I heard a bird call.
It forms all kinds of charm.

The flowers are just right, the moon is full,
And I, alone,
Stepping on the coolness of the night,
Roaming on the mountainside.
Clearly heard,
From the sky,
Sound calling.
No error,
She is Feng Qing, that is Feng Qing.

Come down, Feng Qing. Come down, Feng Qing.

Let me pour out my heartstrings to you:

Because I miss you,

I -

Sleeping restlessly,

Eating without sweet taste,

The spirit is obsessed and confused.

Come down, Feng Qing. Come down, Feng Qing.

I want to tell you:

A hundred fierce birds cannot compare to a fish hawk.

Sincere me,

Like a heavenly flower,

How can green and red grass and trees compare to it!

Come down, Feng Qing. Come down, Feng Qing.

On the wilderness,

The winding paths lead to seclusion,

Let us both,

In the morning and evening, we meet and play together.

Come down, Feng Qing. Come down, Feng Qing.

In my quiet and elegant study,

Sitting face to face and sipping tea,

reading extensively from ancient and modern times,

Let us both

Talk to every corner of the world.

Come down, Feng Qing. Come down, Feng Qing.

Me and you,

Hand in hand to the seaside;

That's where I feel comfortable.

Let us both,

Facing the sea,
Shout the other person's name;
Sincerely request the ocean,
Witness for both of us,
An unchanging oath.

Come down, Feng Qing. Come down, Feng Qing.
Me and you,
Hand in hand to climb the mountains;
There,
The air is fresh and refreshing.
Let us both,
Deeply recognize,
The joy of working together and supporting each other.

Clearly visible,
Feng Qing was filled with joy,
In that high sky,
She shouted loudly:
Come up, Wang Wang. Come up, Wang Wang.
The Heavenly God gave me a cloud and Neon robe,
Please come and appreciate it quickly

Regardless of the pits and hollows,
I fell a few times.
Stepping on the hard steps,
I want to climb up.
Feng Qing asked me:
Please tell me,
Is it beautiful like this?
I......

Not seeing clearly, unable to answer,

Just feel......

Absurd, abrupt, dizzy, lost.

Deeply victimized......

Dark clouds envelop, and monsters descend.

Feng Qing! Feng Qing!

I opened my eyes wide and regained my consciousness,

Suddenly discovered,

You have been drawn into the void.

Instantly,

The stars are out of order,

earth-shattering and heavenly shock,

thunder and lightning,

The wind and rain are miserable,

A tear of sympathy for both of us.

Chapter 24   Hospitalization and Vase

In the spring of the 73rd year of the Republic of China (1984), I intended to cure my childhood hand injury. When I was a child, the last tendon of my left index finger broke due to careless mowing, and it has been curved ever since. The doctor at Taipei Majie Hospital advised me to stay in the hospital for two days. He wanted to remove a small tendon from my left arm and sew on my left index finger.

Before the surgery, the nurse conveyed a message: "Mr. Wang, your junior sister is calling to wish you a speedy recovery. Her name is Leng Na."

I am about to enter the operating room and stand at the door saying to my mother:

"Mom, you wait here. After the operation is completed, you will hear them shouting: 'Wang Wang's family', that's it. You can wait here with peace of mind."

I am lying on the operating bed, under general anesthesia, undergoing surgery.

"Take me to my mother's front to reassure her. Take me to my mother's front to reassure her."

"Wang Wang, wake up. Wang Wang, wake up."

"Take me to my mother's front to reassure her. Take……" I woke up and found that it was my mother who was taking care of me, not anyone else. Opening my eyes wide, I realized that I was no longer in the operating room. The nurse was pushing the gurney slowly towards the ward. It's getting dark too, and my index finger has been cast in plaster.

I was lying on the hospital bed, and Abasan, the caregiver of the adjacent bed, said to my mother, "Your son just woke up. Don't let him move so he won't vomit. Yesterday, after my child had surgery, he only went to the restroom once and came back to vomit."

My mother was about to reply when she noticed a young lady coming to visit. She said:

"I am his junior sister, Leng Na, and I came to see him. I wish him a speedy recovery."

"Please take a seat," my mother said. "Why bother spending money?"

"This is just a small expression of my feelings." Leng Na placed two types of fruits and a bouquet of flowers on the small table.

"Wang Wang, Wang Wang, your junior sister is coming to see you."

"Oh!" I flipped my body slightly and said, "I was under general anesthesia just now and I'm very tired. I just want to sleep." After saying that, I focused on sleeping on my side.

My mother walked out and Leng Na sat waiting; It wasn't until my mother came in again that Leng Na got up and said goodbye.

"What about this bouquet of flowers? Where should I plug it in?"

"I have an empty milk powder can here," said Abasan next to me. "Take it as a vase."

After the placement of the fresh flower milk powder can, my mother turned around and asked:

"What about these fruits?"

"I don't eat the food she gave me."

The next morning, I was full of energy and began reading.

"Take more rest now and study again after returning to school."

"I'm not tired," I closed my book and said, "Mom, if Leng Na comes again in the afternoon, I want to say that a certain girl has also come to see me. I want her to run out angrily."

In the afternoon, I was about to enter the ward from outside and found Leng Na already inside. I took a deep breath and walked in. My mother said:

"She brought a book to give to you."

"......" I didn't speak and sat on the bed, my back against the wall, like a mute.

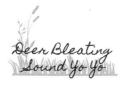

Leng Na took the vase and flowers she had brought to the corridor and inserted the flowers into the vase. After a while, she walked in and stood at the small table sorting out the branches. My mother walked out, leaving me and her.

I lowered my head to sit still, and so did Leng Na. A few minutes later, my mother came in and Leng Na said in Mandarin:

"If you need help with your paper, I can help."

"I think I can handle it. "

"After you are discharged from the hospital, you can call into the office to talk to me, okay?"

"After discharge, I will go to the office."

"Auntie." Leng Na turned around and said to my mother in Minnan dialect: "I made an appointment with my classmate to meet, and I have to leave now."

Leng Na left, and I stared blankly at the flowers, vase, boxed mochi, and a magazine on the table.

I completed the discharge procedures and my third brother-in-law drove to pick me up. My mother walked to the car with a leather bag in one hand and a vase in the other, saying, "This vase is very beautiful, Wang Wang doesn't want it. Let's take it to Yonghe and for you to use."

Returning to Huagang, where spring brings bleak winds and autumn brings bitter rain, I feel helpless. Fortunately, a few younger students came to visit me with fruits, which made me feel warm.

On the eighth day after discharge, Leng Na entered the boys' dormitory and first visited Li Pu. Then, he stopped by to visit me. She opened her eyes wide, looked around, and said:

"Senior, are your hands any better?"

"I'm recovering soon, thank you!" I looked expressionless.

Leng Na sees the situation, leave quickly.

The next day, I met Leng Na on the road and she handed me a book, saying:

"Return the book to you." She asked again, "Where is that vase?"

"My hands haven't recovered yet. The vase is at my third sister's house and I haven't brought it up the mountain."

"That was bought by Feng Qing."

"Did she forget to take it back?"

"No, she deliberately stayed here to give it to you." After walking a little further, Leng Na said, "Senior, can I ask you again about Feng Qing? Do you need my help?"

"No need, I just want to rush to write my paper. I don't plan to pay attention to Feng Qing's matter."

"It's also good."

"Where do you want to go?"

"I want to find Senior Li Pu."

Leng Na and I went upstairs together. As soon as Leng Na saw Li Pu, she immediately shed tears; Sit silently at Li Pu's desk for a few minutes and then say:

"I might resign and go back to my hometown to work as a substitute teacher, but I can't bear to leave Huagang."

"If you can find a permanent job when you go back, it's also good. It's closer to home," Li Pu said later. "When are you planning to go back?"

"These few days."

After Leng Na bid farewell, I called Yonghe and said I wanted to retrieve the vase; Then carefully took it to Huagang.

Passing by the bank of the Hundred Flowers Pond in front of the dance department, I stood transfixed and thought about Feng Qing. I had always been in a state of turmoil and devastation, and couldn't help but feel an inexplicable sadness from the bottom of my heart. At this moment, the breeze was gentle, and a clean and shiny black cat was leisurely sleeping on a large stone. Suddenly looking up, I found green leaves and red flowers, bright and sunny, what a refreshing day. It seems like I haven't experienced this feeling for a long time. How have I spent these past few years? Suddenly, I remembered my paper and flew towards the dormitory. Before rushing for the paper, I wrote a letter to Feng Qing.

February 24th, 1984

Dear Feng Qing:

I never spoke to blame Leng Na, just ignored her. Recently, I was hospitalized for surgery due to an old hand injury.

On the first day, Leng Na came to see me buying flowers and fruits, and saw that I was tired and fell asleep, so she left. The next day, she brought magazines, flowers, vase, and desserts, but I ignored her. She sat for a while, feeling bored and left.

Last night, she returned the books she had borrowed before and asked me, "Where was that vase the other day?" I said, "My hands are not convenient to hold, so I left it at my third sister's house." She told me that you left that vase for me. Subsequently, she went to my classmate and said that she might resign and return to being a substitute teacher in the southern region, but she couldn't bear to leave Huagang and shed a few tears.

My paper progress has seriously fallen behind, let alone my academic and career achievements. I really can't say anything to you. However, for you, I will bravely move forward and become an outstanding person; For you, I need to cultivate moral character, treat people kindlier, and be stricter with myself.

I have a firm belief that there is no second woman in the world who can get it, even though I am a lowly member of society, I am convinced that I have the supreme affection.

The tasks in front of me: writing, submitting for review, finalizing, printing, oral examination...... It will be a long time before I can relax, and now I don't want to be distracted. Let me cherish the vase and pray that the fairy flowers can enter it.

Sincerely,
Wang Wang,

Leng Na has returned to the south for employment, and a student girl met me on campus and said:

"Senior, I heard that you paid the rent for Leng Na to live off campus apartment. Is this true?"

"No such thing, who told you?"

"Really not?"

"Of course not."

"This news has been circulating for a long time, and everyone knows it. Perhaps only you don't know."

Chapter 25   Letters Expressing Sincere Feelings

My emotions have become much calmer, and I must work harder to balance love and career. Since I plan to seek her after finishing my studies, I occasionally write letters in addition to studying hard, so that Feng Qing can have beautiful memories in the future.

Letter 1:

Dear Feng Qing:

You have a pair of beautiful eyebrows, and the excess part below them can be plucked; It grows again every once in a while, and you must trim it again. Doing this will not only make you more beautiful, but it is also said to help you develop a good habit of being careful in everything you do. I don't mind it being trivial, but I am willing to provide it to you.

Sincerely,
Wang Wang

Letter 2:

Dear Feng Qing:

The drizzle floating all over the sky is my mood when I come to Huagang. Why is it that others always hit it off, but I suffer so much?

Walking through the streets of Taipei and stopping in every corner of Huagang, I constantly feel the urge to comment, but there is no confidant beside me.

There is no perfect person in this world. However, as long as we know how to appreciate each other's strengths and tolerate each other's shortcomings, it is not difficult to become happy persons.

My mother loves me very much, and seeing me struggling, she suffered a lot of physical and mental damage. In order to insist on you, I inevitably argue with her; That was a temporary act of unfilial piety, because this insistence was only aimed at obtaining a good girl who could sincerely respect my mother. Indeed, "If you love my house, you will also love the birds next to it." That's a smart person. I hope you know how to cherish her.

There is a kind of person who indulges in enjoyment all day long, but never loses virtue; Greedy and insatiable, yet able to benefit the crowd; He is full of vitality, and when people approach him, they can feel a gentle breeze, that is the scholar in the library. I hope we can join hands and enter this great paradise on earth.

Sincerely,

Wang Wang

Letter 3:

Dear Feng Qing:

What is sincere love? It seems like a kind of holy and noble friendship. Who would have expected that when implemented, it is so simple and ordinary that everyone has the capital to achieve it? However, it seems that there are not many people who want to taste the taste of sincerity, because people often regard multiple goals as enjoying erotic pleasures.

Han Feizi said: Most queens and princes hope that the king will die soon, because "If the queen is favored, her son will be embraced by the king". The queen will inevitably age, and one day, the king will turn to doting on her young and beautiful concubine, and gradually distance himself from the queen; The

Crown Prince is also constantly worried about couldn't inherit the throne. If the king dies early, the queen can not only do whatever she wants, but also her son can smoothly inherit the throne. From this perspective, the king is almost the saddest person in the world, he cannot even get true love from a woman.

Sincerely,

Wang Wang

Letter 4:

Dear Feng Qing:

The "*Zhiyuelu*" (Collection of Pointing to the Moon) records a passage from Master Weixin of Qingyuan, saying: "I, an old monk, thirty years ago, when I was not meditating in Zen, I saw that mountains were mountains and water was water. Later on, when I personally saw knowledge, there was an entrance; seeing mountains were not mountains, and water was not water. Now I have a resting place. According to the past, seeing mountains are only mountains, and seeing water is only water." In a few words, he explained the level of cultivation. Yes, for example, the phrase "patriotism" spoken by elementary school students is vastly different from the phrase "patriotism" spoken by Yue Fei and Wen Tianxiang.

In terms of emotions, there are also three realms. The first one is self attachment and ignorance: they live in drunken dreams and muddle through their lifeless lives. The second type is lost and disoriented: they seem to have a good understanding of style, but their brilliance is like a flash in the pan; His words are as firm as iron, but in fact, they are like soil and cannot stand the test. The third type is the true self and the realization of the Tao: they truly understand the true essence of emotions, which is the realm of "Ask the world, what is love? It can even make people give each other their lives"; Being able to reach this level can be said to be that this life has not been a waste of time. "Without using Qingse to play the music of Nishang and Yuyi, ordinary secular dreams would not know the lofty and long-lasting nature of the Crane Dream." Among all the intellectuals with pure conduct, noble moral character and magnanimous spirit, who does not have ideals in their hearts? Who wants to stay in a state of clinging to the flesh without a spirit, or wandering without a master?

The common people often suffer from various forms of ridicule in the world, and show a hypocritical face or act hypocritically; People with conscience and blood often feel that the word 'sincerity' is not common anymore. The true love has been lost and disappeared due to facing many wrong paths. Modern men and women are also influenced by utilitarianism in their relationships, resulting in many couples having different dreams even when they sleep together; On the surface, it looks very compatible, but in fact, it is the separation between the divine soul and the body; this phenomenon makes people exclaim endlessly.

Zhang Jiuling's poem: "I wish a pure white heart would always be there and never be stained black. "Xunzi said, "Zhilan is born in the deep forest and will not be unwilling to fragrance because no one appreciates it." I want to firmly grasp the word "sincerity" in the fallen era. Looking for a woman who aligns perfectly with my thoughts and stays together; Always treat each other with courtesy and blend into the world of art; Carefully experience the joy of true love, without showing off to the world.

Sincerely,
Wang Wang

Letter 5:

Dear Feng Qing:

In the industrial and commercial society where science and technology are advancing by leaps and bounds, people are busy and lacking in spiritual life, and all living beings are gradually bound by machines. Su Dongpo said, "I often feel resentful that this body does not belong to me. When will I forget about the busy life of competing for fame and wealth?" Monk Lingche said: "When people meet, they all agree that it is good to retire from office. But in fact, have you ever seen

a person really retreating to the forest?" They saw that human beings are busy and struggling on the one hand, but also long for rest and enjoyment. The contradiction between them is truly impressive.

I aspire to immerse myself in the embrace of nature, savoring the delights of "the yard, pond, pear blossoms, and willow catkins all bathed in the moonlight like water, and the gentle breeze blowing in a realm of tranquility and lingering emotions" and "the sparse shadows of plum blossoms, slanting across the shallow water, with their delicate fragrance floating under the moonlight at dusk". But it is undeniable that material things can facilitate and enrich life, but they must complement spiritual life. Therefore, I am also willing to work tirelessly to create comfortable living conditions.

Tree flowers are blossoming, some drifting towards the mat, and some falling into cesspits. The ancients used this kind of thing as a metaphor for the fate of life. I believe that falling flowers have no independent ability, and humans, as long as they are willing to work hard, can achieve their ideals. So, our future should be optimistic.

Sincerely,
Wang Wang

Card 1:

The women around me will sincerely love and respect me, because I respect them with a gentle and dignified attitude, and even more because I firmly dedicate all my emotions to my wife alone.

Card 2:

In pursuit of the ideals of truth, goodness, and beauty, I have persisted to this day. I hope we have a good relationship that will last and strengthen.

Chapter 26   Before and After Oral Exam

A week before my master's oral exam, I saw the poster of the Dance Class 3 exhibition. I am very busy, but when encountering Feng Qing's dance exhibition, I must overcome difficulties and go to watch it.

In the morning, I went to the photo studio next to the school to rent a camera and prepare to take photos.

Thirty minutes before the dance show, I had already taken my seat and waited, holding a small program booklet and a camera in my hand. First, I carefully searched for Feng Qing's name and knew that she would appear in four programs: Third, Pioneer. Sixth, random thoughts. Twelfth, beginning. Seventeenth, spring outing. In addition, the eighth program "Afternoon" is choreographed by Feng Qing.

The show started, and whenever Feng Qing performed, I would rush to the bottom of the stage to take photos, carefully capturing the beautiful shots. Feng Qing did not participate in any programs where male students participated, which is also a major feature. However, it seems that etiquette has narrowed Feng Qing's creative path and constrained her artistic expression. Whether in choreography or dancing, Feng Qing did not fully unleash her potential like others, which is a bit regrettable. For example, her classmates were able to dance "Nightmares of Nuns" and "The innocence of two children" with great excitement.

"Spring outing" is the last program, and at the moment when the music is about to end, the twelve girls are performing even harder. They took turns entering behind the curtain and then taking turns appearing again. Time and time again, Feng Qing stood behind the curtain, with only his head exposed, looking at me in the audience. My eyes met hers, but she didn't have a smile.

After the dance, I sent the negatives for development. What is incredible is that most of them were failed photos; there were almost no very satisfactory photos. I have taken many photos during the day with few problems; I never expected that such stage photography in the dark and with lights still requires professionalism and training. I am basically a layman in this regard.

My master's thesis oral exam passed smoothly, and Professor Jin from Taiwan University said to Director Pan, "This student is very outstanding, and I recommend that he be admitted to the doctoral program!"

"Okay, okay," Director Pan readily agreed.

In the evening, I selected a master's thesis, mentioned a few words, and wrote another letter to Feng Qing.

Dear Feng Qing:

The doctoral entrance exam will be held on July 5th, I have already registered; No matter how the entrance exam results are, I will notify you.

Please find attached the master's thesis and photos.

Sincerely,
Wang Wang

I sent out my paper and stayed at home for a few days. Later on, when I returned to school, I went to the uncle in the mail room to check the registered account book. Feng Qing had already stamped and received my master's thesis, and I was filled with joy.

On June 27th, I helped my classmates take a taxi to pick up Professor Wang to the school as a committee member for the thesis oral examination.

Professor Wang got off the car first and walked into the building. I paid the driver and then hurriedly chased after him. As I walked to the office of the dance department, I was about to follow Professor Wang, but I suddenly stopped and thought for a moment, "Isn't that Feng Qing?" Then I turned around and saw clearly that it was indeed Feng Qing standing in front of the bulletin board. I took a step or two back and said: "Hi, Feng Qing."

Feng Qing didn't speak, moved one or two steps, entered the dressing room, faced me, and stood with his head down. I followed to the entrance of the dressing room and saw her dressed in white. I found that she had indeed arranged her eyebrows more beautifully. The gentle and quiet appearance resembles a gentle little white rabbit. I said:

"My classmate is taking his master's thesis oral exam later. I just helped him pick up the teacher and I have to go upstairs now." I quickly ran upstairs and caught up with Professor Wang.

Chapter 27   Shock

On July 5, 1984, the entrance examination for the doctoral program ended in the afternoon. In the evening, I called Feng Qing and a stranger answered.

"My name is Wang Wang. May I ask if Feng Qing is there?"

"She's not here. She wants me to tell you that she already has a boyfriend. Please don't look for her."

"May I ask who you are?"

"It's her roommate."

I hung up the phone, got furious, and immediately wrote a letter.

Feng Qing:

Your roommate told me that you already have a boyfriend and suggested that I don't need to look for you anymore. If this is a fact, thank you for not revealing it until I finished my exam; In the past days, it always kept my emotions calm. If you don't actually have another boyfriend, then undoubtedly, you have already paved the way out now. I'm sorry, I failed this exam and I just want to move my things home and wait for enlistment.

I don't need to retrieve the photo, you can tear it up yourself.

Wang Wang

In the evening, I arrived at Yonghe and learned that my mother had fallen and been injured. She was hospitalized for half a month and was discharged only two days ago. In order to keep me focused on preparing for the exam, she refused to let me know.

Quickly, my third sister, nephew, and I returned to Nantou together. Entering the house, I sat by the bedside, tears streaming down like rain.

"Mom, why didn't you let me know after being hospitalized for so long?"

My mother also shed tears. When she wiped away her tears, she said, "I'm almost recovered now. You finished the exam, didn't you?"

"I have finished the exam and will have to wait for two weeks before the rankings are released."

"How is that girl from Taoyuan now?"

"I don't understand her, I need some time to figure it out."

"When going out, don't compete with others, and be more relaxed. It's easy for us to find girls. It's okay if she comes or not; there are so many girls in the world."

"I know."

"If she is destined to eat from our family, this matter will naturally come to fruition. No matter who she is, as long as she is our daughter-in-law, we will love her. Don't worry."

Returning to school, I felt very down. Through the phone, I asked them to convey to Feng Qing that if she decides not to socialize with me, I plan to return the vase. She immediately agreed, and soon, I took the vase sent by Leng Na in February this year and walked to the roadside outside the dance department. She personally came out and without saying a word, took back the vase.

On July 10th, my anger subsided and I couldn't help but write to Feng Qing.

Dear Feng Qing:

I have always believed that you are a beautiful girl, but your thoughts are elusive. Perhaps my temper is too bad and I often make things uncontrollable.

No matter what, you can communicate and discuss with me calmly, but you always give up trying. What is the reason?

Several teachers expressed optimism about my application for the doctoral program, and the list will be released soon on the 18th; If I pass the exam, I will notify you; If I unfortunately fail, you can refuse me, and I have no complaints.

Sincerely,
Wang Wang

On July 18th, the results of the doctoral entrance examination were announced. After reading the list, I called Gongguan and Feng Qing answered the phone.

"I passed the exam."

"Congratulations. Wang Wang, I really have a boyfriend now. Please don't come to me."

After standing for a while, I said, "I want to talk to you in person, okay?"

"No, I'm not free."

The next day, I called Gongguan and her younger brother answered the phone, saying:

"I am his younger brother, and my sister hopes you don't call. She has been in a bad mood lately, and she said she only wants to live an ordinary life in the future.

On the 25th, Feng Qing sent a letter and returned the photo, stating:

Wang Wang:

I really have a boyfriend, I told you from the beginning, but you never believed me.

You are good to me, of course I know. Because we haven't started yet, there is no sadness to say.

I know you are a very excellent boy, please don't be sad; Around you, there are many girls who you can pursue. I wish you happiness, and I also ask you not to write again.

Sincerely,
Feng Qing

This statement is certainly clear enough, but I still want to see her once, which will make me feel more at ease. Her mother answered the phone and told me:

"She really has a boyfriend. Do you think it's necessary to have a conversation? She's kind-hearted and afraid of hurting others."

"I know she's fine."

"Yes, if you really need to meet and talk, Feng Qing said that she would only go with her boyfriend."

"……" I hesitated for a moment and said, "I confirm that I will go to Taipei on August 13th. Could you please advise her to come out and meet at the entrance of Taiwan University at 6pm on the 14th?"

"I'll just tell her, it's not certain if she will go."

Chapter 28   Second Date

On August 13, 1984 (the 73rd year of the Republic of China), at 8 o'clock in the morning, I was preparing to depart from Nantou. According to normal circumstances, every morning, my father went to work in the field. Today, in order to see me go north, he stayed at home. Mother prepared four fruits and went to the hall for devout worship. I started wearing socks and shoes, and my father was sitting, standing, and wandering in the next room, with anxiety all written on his face. My father said, "I think there shouldn't have been any results from this trip. So, don't stay in Taipei too long, come back as soon as possible." As he walked out of the house, he walked in again and said, "Based on my speculation, she should have a boyfriend……"

"Dad, there's no need to say more. No matter what the outcome of this trip to Taipei is, it doesn't matter. You've been so kind to me, and I know it very well. Please rest assured that if I fail, I won't take it too hard. I will definitely cherish myself." I smiled and comforted him with ease.

Before going to the appointment, I went to the home of the third elder sister in Yonghe. The third brother-in-law said to me: "Feng Qing is a very powerful character. I knew it when I listened to her talk on the phone. She said

that your thoughts and actions were deviant from the beginning. She had no intention of further development with you, and she had repeatedly explained it to you, but you didn't believe it, and it got deeper and deeper; This has nothing to do with her. She wants to solemnly declare that she has already said she has a boyfriend, but you don't believe it. If you continue to be stubborn, don't blame her for being impolite. I feel sorry for you after hearing her words. Your appearance has become so ugly, haven't you realized it to this day? Normally, I see that you are very good at talking and reading, but you have a lot of difficulties when it comes to falling in love. Don't say I'm farting. When I was young, I had the ability to drive young ladies around in two or three days, and I made several friends. Which one wasn't obedient and considerate?"

I have no intention of refuting those accusations; Even if I did, I'm afraid they wouldn't understand.

At 4:45 pm on August 14th, I arrived at the entrance of Taiwan University. At 6:10, I called Taoyuan and Feng Qing's mother answered the phone.

"May I ask Aunt, will Feng Qing come?"

"Yes, she said they would go."

"Thank you, Aunt."

At 6:20, Feng Qing appeared in the distance and walked towards me with a boy. She was wearing very simple clothes and jeans; His clothes are also simple, and they look very suitable for each other.

"I'm sorry, we're late." The boy who greeted me with a smile had a clear and handsome appearance, and I was filled with joy.

"I have just arrived."

"Haven't eaten yet? Let's go!" Feng Qing gracefully led the way and entered the restaurant.

I remember my first date with Feng Qing was on April 19, 1982, when we sat down and had a meal in the restaurant next to the school. After dinner, we sat together on the grass next to a villa, about five steps apart. She wrapped her hands around her chest and chatted with me as a gentleman and a lady. Next came a long and intermittently dark period of three years and four months, and I didn't know if I seemed to be treated like a demon or a rogue. During this period, the distance between me and her was infinite. Today, it was not easy for me to have a second table meeting with her. I sat on one side and she and he sat on the other side.

Why do I have to sit there for so long when the things I originally wanted to confirm have already been confirmed? I must stay here to complete the entire program, which is a courtesy and obligation.

Suddenly, I separated my body from the truth self. My body is murky, and what it says about beauty may not necessarily be beauty; If it speaks well, it may not necessarily be good; Its smile is a stiff skin smile; My body is left here, just supporting the scene and responding perfunctorily. And my true self is an eternal existence, true and not illusory. At this moment, my true self has lifted itself from its obscurity and risen to a place of freedom, comfort, and tranquility. There is indeed someone or something mentioned in the room, but I am simply absent-minded.

The waiter brought the meal over, and Feng Qing's boyfriend said:

"Are you planning to serve in the military first and then pursue a doctoral degree?"

"Yes. Military service is a major issue, and it is always not good if it is not resolved first and weighed on my heart."

"You've never worked outside before, right?"

"No, I have only participated in the editing work of the school's publishing department, and I am only considered a part-time student."

"In the history of modern Chinese literature, articles like Shen Congwen are considered good."

"Well, there are many books available on the roadside."

"Do you live in Nantou and grow tea?"

"Planting one or two hectares, our reputation is not as famous as Lugu."

"Last time I visited Lugu for inspection, I also learned how to make tea from them and found it very interesting."

"Making tea is also a subject of learning."

At this point, both sides remained silent for a moment.

"In fact, when it comes to making girlfriends, it's inevitable to encounter setbacks and feel sad for a while; like I used to...... "

"You don't," I interrupted him, but immediately turned into a faint smile and said confidently," Because you're very handsome."

At this moment, the scene was a bit awkward.

"Have you watched the broadcast of the Olympics recently?" Feng Qing broke the deadlock.

"I watched some. We got the bronze medal."

"Louis is really not easy, he won the gold medal on all four sides."

"Westerners have a better physique than us. Like last month's Jones Cup basketball match, the Chinese team ranked seventh for men and fifth for women. Our physique is really not suitable for comparing basketball with foreigners."

"In fact, from a medical perspective, a person's bones cannot be too long. If they are too long, they often become sore in old age. Like many basketball stars, in their later years, there are more bone problems than the average person."

I didn't answer, thinking to myself: I only have 178 centimeters, and the problem caused by the long bones he mentioned should have nothing to do with me.

Feng Qing and her boyfriend had finished eating, but I still had a lot left and had no appetite at all, so I put down my chopsticks and said:

"That's all I need to eat."

"Do you need to talk to her outside?"

"No need," I replied briskly.

Feng Qing smiled and secretly twisted his thigh with her hand as a protest.

"Let's take a seat at the bookstore."

The three of us walked out and Feng Qing asked, "Are you going back to Nantou tomorrow?"

"I'll finish collecting the things on the mountain and leave."

Take a short walk, take the elevator upstairs, and enter a bookstore; Standing at the counter is Feng Qing's classmate - Xiao Mei.

There are many small tables in the bookstore, with tatami placed around them, which is a place for customers to read, drink, and chat.

The three of us sat around a table and ordered a cold drink. Feng Qing went to a distant corner to find a young foreign man who was Feng Qing's English-speaking partner. Later, Xiao Mei also came to sit around.

Feng Qing and Xiao Mei introduced me with a smile to the foreigner, saying that I had passed the entrance examination for the doctoral program at the Literature Research Institute and planned to serve in the military and become an officer first. The foreigner also mentioned his willingness to learn Chinese and talked about Feng Qing's graduation trip next year.

At first, I managed to squeeze a smile and perfunctory the scene, but later I felt mentally exhausted and could only sit there expressionless. Sometimes I looked at Feng Qing with a helpless gaze. At the beginning, Feng Qing spoke English with a lively and joyful expression, but gradually restrained and turned into silence before finally leaving the table. Xiao Mei followed and withdrew.

"It's a bit late, I should go back now," I suggested first, still with a humble and polite attitude.

The foreigner walked back to his original position. Feng Qing's boyfriend made the payment, and Feng Qing stood in front of the counter, smiling again. Say:

"You go first, I'll stay here."

"Goodbye!" I saluted her and then took the elevator down with"him" to the roadside. He reached out to me and said, "We are friends."

"Yes," I shook hands with him and said, "Goodbye."

Fate is really good at playing tricks on people. I just feel that this matter has been delayed for too long and takes too much effort. Even with extremely firm determination and perseverance, I still have to declare failure in the end. On April 19, 1982, Feng Qing and I went on a separate date, that's all. Feng Qing wrote in a letter a few days ago (July 25, 1984): "Because we haven't started yet, there's no sadness to speak of." If we use the timer to calculate, we are just two people who have been dating and talking for less than 2 hours. So, with such time data, she calls me a "stranger". How does she know what kind of personality I am? But how could someone who only has 2 hours to meet and talk to consume years of my mental energy and occupy the space of my diaries? These calculation methods can't help but make me feel sad. I don't know what she really thinks in her heart.

After my second date with her, everything finally returned to normal and calm. Apart from the manuscripts of some previous letters, several diaries were completely destroyed by me, and I can only declare the end here. How many relatives and friends have mocked me behind my back because of this matter, how many rumors have slandered my personality and emotional life, and some people think that my ability to handle things is poor. I really can't find any friends to clarify, and I don't care anymore.

I carefully looked at the image of Buddha and Bodhisattva in Cave 45 of Mogao Grottoes in Dunhuang, Gansu Province. There was a monkey in the lower left and right corners. Buddhism uses the term "heart ape mind horse" to describe sentient beings who are unstable in their minds and unable to hold themselves. However, in fact, all living beings have the Buddha nature of being calm and aware. Therefore, I combine these concepts into: "Heart ape

mind horse, calmness knows emptiness." When I find it difficult to let go, I meditate: "Heart ape mind horse, calmness knows emptiness. Follow fate, let go; let go, follow fate."

But I have always been strong, I am aboveboard, I have done my best, and I do not owe anything to my own sincere heart. From now on, I still need to keep this sincere heart, and in the future, marriage and life will definitely be happy and joyful. I have always had deep confidence.

Chapter 29   Completing Military Service and Attending a Doctoral Program

I joined the army and served as a second lieutenant officer at the Army Academy. I taught Chinese language courses and was also responsible for arranging course schedules; Until being discharged from the military.

During my time in the military, I felt very calm and fulfilling. Actually, there are not many people like me, because every weekend or holiday, I stay in the camp to read books, and reading addiction has almost become a special symbol of myself. Most officers of military academies also know that I am such a "strange person"; As for what they think in their hearts, I am not actually interested in speculating. Before I was about to be discharged from the military, my immediate supervisor, Colonel Huang, requested my superiors to give me a certificate of commendation, which was issued by General Jiang Zhongling, the Commander in Chief of the Army. So, what is the significance of rewarding me for? I'm not sure either.

In September 1986, in the 75th year of the Republic of China, I was discharged from the military and returned to Huagang to study for a doctoral degree. I lived in the dormitory of Dazhuangguan. Feng Qing has graduated from university and it is said that she has already got married.

On October 26th, I stood in front of the girls' dormitory in the next building waiting for my junior sister to pick up her book. After only two minutes, I suddenly realized that Feng Qing was standing next to the gate. She walked out step by step and saw me. She was startled and immediately turned inside. I was also shocked and thought to myself, "Isn't she already graduated? Why is she still in school?" After a while, Feng Qing walked out again, smiling and whispering to another girl standing in front of me; I am temporarily looking at the other side. It wasn't until we gave each other a real glance that she walked into the dormitory.

My junior sister walked out of the dormitory and finished discussing business with me. I asked her to inquire about the name of the dance department assistant. A few days later, my junior sister told me that the teaching assistant in the dance department is Feng Qing, who lives in room 204 of the dormitory.

I have always had a question in my heart, what exactly did Leng Na say that made Feng Qing angrily move home from the mountain. Therefore, during working hours, I called the dance department office and Feng Qing answered the phone with a friendly attitude. I said I wanted to talk to her when I had time, and she generously agreed. After hanging up the phone and thinking for a while, I feel that if I still want to ask what Leng Na said before, it's really meaningless; Moreover, she has a happy marriage now, that would be great, and I really don't have a word to say to her; So, I haven't talked to her since then. Entering another new semester, if the news is correct, I heard she has resigned.

I am pursuing a doctoral program while also serving as a university

Chinese language teacher. Some of the content of the student's essay touched me deeply, for example, a girl wrote:

> Since I grew up a bit and became more sensible, I have found it difficult to manage a marriage.

> My father is often away from home due to work reasons. Even if he is transferred to a place not far from home, he almost returns late every day. Whenever I am awakened by my mother's scolding, I know that my father has returned. If she doesn't get married, she won't be hindered by our few children. Sometimes, I feel sorry for my mother. Although she never shed tears in front of us, I secretly cried for her several times.

> For ordinary and broken past events, it's better to say that I'm quite used to it than not caring. I have asked myself if I want to have a fixed life or relationship between the two sexes in the future, but there is no answer every time. I may be very eager, but I am also very afraid to have it because I cannot believe that there will be eternal things, and the relationship between everyone or everything is so fragile.

There is a boy who is also in a very painful relationship and feeling very low. I take the position of a counselor and have the obligation to enlighten him, but I cannot handle my own emotional problems. What can I do to help him? Even though I felt a bit uneasy, I still brought him here and solemnly preached:

> "The ancients once had a metaphor: men are big trees, women are vines; Big trees only need to grow tall and strong, and naturally there will be vines coming to climb. If it not only fails to grow well itself, but also twists itself to entangle the vine, it will inevitably end up losing both. So, if a boy cannot win the hearts of a girl, it's better to reflect on oneself: 'Perhaps my achievements or knowledge are not good enough, and I need to work harder to strengthen myself and achieve myself.' So, future success should be as simple as if the water arrived and the canal formed."

Chapter 30   The deadline for choosing a spouse has arrived

"The frozen pool never ripples." I am no longer interested in dating. I graduated from the doctoral program after four years, and in August 1980, I officially became a full-time teacher. How did I procrastinate and cope with the marital pressure from my parents? Perhaps it can only be described as vague. I vaguely remember saying to my family, "As long as you don't make a decision for me, I'm willing to go on blind dates as many times as you want." Under this principle, if someone wants to ask me, "How many blind dates have you gone through?" I don't have an answer because it's too many to count; And almost all of them were immediately forgotten after a meeting.

Until one day when I went home, my mother said, "Your father goes to work in the fields. Whenever he thinks of getting so old and not getting a daughter-in-law, his hands and feet are even soft, and he can't even lift a hoe or sickle. Do you know how many times he cried secretly?"

My father came back from work in the fields and officially had an appointment with me. He said, "If someone with a shorter life has left now, can they still see their daughter-in-law and grandchildren?" He also said, "I have a private question for you. Are you having a physical or physiological problem that you dare not let us know, so you have been using procrastination methods to delay this matter?"

"That's not the case, don't think nonsense."

Quickly, I calmly said to my mother, "I am very sorry for you. I should have gotten married. In your impression, which girl do you think is the best we have seen? I am willing to socialize with her." I thought to myself, "As long as that woman is willing to marry me, she is destined to be very happy. Because my heart is pure."

Chapter 31　Marry

My third sister quickly jumped out and introduced me to a teacher at Taipei Business College (now National Taipei Business University). She obtained a master's degree from Nagoya University in Japan and later became my wife.

At first, I heard that she is a Scorpio, and I had some doubts because it was said that Aquarius and Scorpio are not suitable for pairing. Later on, I thought: if one's character is good, everything will be good; As long as we treat each other sincerely, there may be differences in our traits, but there should be no reason for being difficult to get along with.

My engagement and marriage were all decided in a hurry, like taking an express train. I got married on January 16th, 1992 (December 12th, 1991, lunar calendar). Our whole family, including we newly married couple, didn't even think or mention a word about our honeymoon trip. On the first day of the Lunar New Year, I used a motorcycle to drive my wife around the village. The upper half of the village was Luming Village, and the lower half was Buxia Village, allowing her to feel what kind of rural place she had married into. Let her know that besides teaching in Taipei, she is already a rural woman. I watched her embrace everything in front of her with a joyful heart, and the entire half hour of sightseeing was unforgettable for a lifetime; That was the sincerest, determined, grateful, and happy honeymoon trip!

Shortly after, we took out a loan to buy a house behind the Zhongzheng Memorial Hall on Xinyi Road in Taipei City. In order not to burden us, my father helped me pay off the mortgage in one go. However, after marriage, I transferred to teach in the central and southern regions and lived in the school dormitory. I had to travel north and south every week to meet my wife.

My doctoral thesis supervisor, Professor Pan Zhonggui, wrote a calligraphy piece for me and I hung it on the wall. The general idea is as follows:

> All kinds of organizations must have a designated leader; Only in the family, couples are equal; The wisdom and personality of people are naturally different, and the way to achieve equality and unity is through mutual respect; If you have the same personality, you can love each other, but if you have different personalities, you need to know how to respect each other. Things at home and outdoors can be managed separately, and the qualities of strictness and kindness can complement each other. Both division of labor and cooperation make couples feel like one person; Over time, couples have become more familiar with each other, helping each other, achieving each other's goals, working together with one heart, and cooperating sincerely.

I remember when I was in the second grade of elementary school, I used a pair of bamboo dustpans to pick up pineapples and put two on one side. Sometime later, I switched to bamboo baskets to pick out pineapples. A few years later, my shoulder picking ability was no less than that of an adult. At first, every time I saw adults working for half an hour, their entire clothes were soaked through, and everyone was like this, while my clothes were still dry; At that time, I couldn't help but admire them from the bottom of my heart. It wasn't until I grew up a bit and my workload were equal to that of an adult that I realized how easy it was to get soaked in sweat all over my body. Our entire head is wrapped in a large cloth towel, and wearing a large bamboo hat on our head, we always feel cold all over and not afraid of the sun - that's a wonderful feeling. During the summer vacation in high school, I had great strength and set a record. Without the help of workers, I personally picked 8000 catties of pineapples in one day.

⊕ ⊕ ⊕

I started teaching in university, and my father once chatted with friends in the village and said: "In the past, the working environment was so poor and the tools were so difficult to use. We have been enduring it year after year. Nowadays, the working environment has improved, and there is no need to raise water buffalo. Instead, we use cultivators. Now we don't have to carry heavy loads on our shoulders, but we have a single wheeled handcart to use; You can also drive a motor truck to transport crops. But with such a good working environment, people are getting old!" In order to eliminate my father's regret and also because I believe that exercise is beneficial for health, I do not dissuade my father from continuing to work in the fields. My wife and I usually don't live in Nantou, but during the summer vacation, there was a big harvest of pineapples in Nantou. We both had to go home and help, which was a very tiring and happy time.

The hands of labor are noble hands. Diligence is my wife's greatest characteristic. Because she is busy with the children's affairs every day, she has to go to bed very late, but she also has to wake up at 5 o'clock every morning, cook meals, put clothes into the washing machine, feed the children, air the clothes, and then wrap herself in sunscreen clothes, put on gloves, and help carry pineapples in the field; Mainly pushing a single wheeled cart to push the harvested pineapples onto a transport truck. Due to the high production volume, sometimes it is even necessary to work until 4 pm to complete the task; As for lunch, simply order lunch boxes and sit by the field for a simple meal. During the day, sweat alternates between dry and wet cycles, achieving a great workout effect. My wife always works wholeheartedly, not only without any complaints, but also enjoys it, which is truly admirable.

Sometimes it is not convenient for me to go back to my hometown to help. I will invite my nephews to help me carry pineapples. They are tall and strong college students, but they often work and shout hard while consuming a lot of physical strength. After returning home, they would tell my sister, "I finally know the reason why my uncle studies so hard."

After I had been married for three years, my wife helped me give birth to three little boys, which completely relieved my parents of their worries over the years and made them satisfied. Someone met my wife on the Taipei campus and asked in surprise, "Why do I see you pregnant every year when I meet you?" Outsiders may not know that such a small brother group is especially easy for parents. They take care of themselves, not stick to adults all day long, but can build deep brotherhood from childhood.

In order for children to have beetles and unicorn immortals to watch, I planted a light wax tree in the field outside the wall, and within a few years, I saw results. Later, I found out that children are more interested in television and toys; The person who likes to watch beetles and unicorns is actually the one who was closely guarded as a child and didn't have the opportunity to explore around at night like other children, carrying a flashlight. It's me.

After two or three years of marriage, I once stayed at my father-in-law's house in Kaohsiung for three days during the Chinese New Year. My father-in-law drove me and my wife out to do things, and I sat in the front seat while my wife sat in the back seat. My father-in-law said to me, "When teaching at school, there shouldn't be any emotional issues between male teachers and female students, but those things that happen between colleagues are relatively okay." I was surprised by this sentence, and my wife never said a word, and I didn't look back at her expression. We remained silent, and the topic shifted accordingly. Afterwards, I did not have any romantic relationships with my female colleagues at school. My father-in-law thought I might be like other men, but he was actually wrong.

My parents-in-law gave birth to a total of two sons and two daughters, all of whom studied in Japan and obtained master's or doctorate degree. The whole family was very kind and courteous, and they all treated me like a distinguished guest. I was very touched and felt that this was a great blessing for me.

Tuesday, August 5, 1997. I took my mother and child to Nantou City to see a dentist. I parked the car on the roadside, my mother was with the child in the dental clinic, and I sat alone in the back seat of my car reading. Suddenly, a car chase and collision occurred in the distance behind me. The driver who caused the accident panicked and drove away, chasing and colliding along the road. He came to the left rear of my car and continued to collide with a small car, then tilted to the side and dented the left rear luggage compartment of my car. The lampshade also broke, and he stopped because it got stuck; I was hit hard and felt a considerable vibration. The police immediately chased up and recorded the time of the collision as 4:30 pm. I left my personal information and negotiated with the perpetrator for repair and compensation matters. Subsequently, I drove my mother and child home for twelve kilometers and arrived at home, only to find that my wife had just cleaned the rice and water on the floor. She said:

"I was washing rice and preparing to cook dinner, but suddenly 'touched' and the whole pot of rice and water spilled all over the ground."

"Do you remember when it was overturned."

"At 4:30, I don't know why this is happening."

My wife is a Japanese language teacher.

Chapter 32 Confirmation of Constellation Views

In 2012, there was a Libra female student in the in-service training class who performed exceptionally well. She believed that Aquarius and Libra people were the most compatible. It would be true to say that talking to each other was very congenial. Gradually, her speaking style in class was also different from that of ordinary students. For example, in a Tai Chi Chuan class, she would directly say, "My period has arrived." Other students couldn't help but be surprised and probably would find it unbelievable. She once said to me alone, "Because I am a fish, you cannot see my tears." She has invited me to dinner several times on the grounds of thanking teachers or asking questions; Sometimes she also invites her classmates to participate. She drove me to the restaurant several times. Sometimes, I think from the bottom of my heart, Libra is so considerate to Aquarius!

At 8 a.m. on March 20, 2013, Director Li of the School of Engineering stood under the banyan tree in front of the liberal arts building. I was about to enter the liberal arts building when he stopped me and said, "Please wait a moment. I have something to tell you."

● ● ●

"What's the matter?"

"You had a dinner party last night, didn't you?"

"Yes, Professor Xu from Xiamen University came to give a speech yesterday, and then several of our teachers had dinner with him."

"I know a person with a high level of spiritual practice who can see things that ordinary people cannot see. A while ago, he saw our school's teacher ○○○ on the road and immediately concluded that he was about to get into trouble. Sure enough, within a few days, this teacher appeared on the Peach News page of Apple Daily. Last night, while the seven of you were having dinner, my friend said to me, 'That one (is talking about you), there may be some emotional issues lately.' Therefore, based on my colleague's position, I think I should make a special trip to remind you to pay attention. If you like, I can arrange for you to meet him."

"Is there such a thing?" I thought for a second or two and then said, "Okay, thank you for coming and telling me." I saluted him and walked into the teaching building.

Director Li has never had any conversation with me before. He and his family used to live in the school dormitory. In a nine-story building, I don't know which floor he lives on, but I occasionally meet him on the road below the dormitory and nod, that's all. Later, their entire family moved out of the dormitory, perhaps buying a new house off campus!

Yesterday, when dining at the restaurant by the lotus pond, the tables were full and the guests were talking loudly, as if it was a bit noisy. I didn't even realize that Director Li was also dining on site. Unexpectedly, a so-called "expert" could give a preventive warning to a stranger like me. Although I had never acted recklessly, at that time was I covered in dark clouds or yellow? This is incredibly magical! I did not consider arranging to meet with the experts, as such shameful emotional troubles should be resolved by myself.

● ● ●

On the weekend, I drove north to reunite with my family. I truthfully told my wife about the content of Director Li's conversation with me. Her response was very clear, just like the decisive poem written by Zhuo Wenjun back to Sima Xiangru in the Han Dynasty: "I want someone who is dedicated and will not abandon me even when it comes to white heads." Soon after, my wife resolutely applied for retirement and went south to live with me in the dormitory. She started working as a teaching assistant and later became a Japanese language teacher. She has served in public service for 25 years and has met the retirement requirements. She is so willing to retire without any reluctance, usually watches TV mainly on Japanese dramas, mainland dramas, health and wellness programs, and Buddhist lectures. She often shares her experiences in listening to scriptures with me or talks about Buddhism to me.

Regarding the Libra girl issue, I solemnly reviewed and reflected on various aspects of my long-term marital life situation:

Although my wife is a Scorpio and according to relevant books, this sign is not suitable for pairing with Aquarius, I evaluate her from four perspectives: she loves this family, loves the people in my family, deeply loves me, and does her best to take care of our children; Having these four touching behaviors at the same time, she is certainly an excellent wife and mother.

We do adopt the principle of "division of labor according to the nature of work" in the way of husband and wife living together, with me doing the heavy work and her doing the light work. I grew up in a hardworking farming family. Whenever I have free time, I like DIY, repairing this and that. But because I was the only boy in my family since I was young, with four elder sisters and one younger sister, I tend to have a spoiled and dependent personality. My wife is the eldest daughter in the family and has been managing her younger

brother and sister since childhood in Kaohsiung, so she tends to have a family oriented and management oriented personality. After getting married, I received meticulous care from her, which may be beyond ordinary people's imagination. At breakfast every day, boiled eggs, milk, Mantou, fruit and coffee are served in order, and then Group B and lutein are placed. I am asked to take one after breakfast. During this time in the early morning, all I did was exercise, eat big meals, and watch TV.

During dinner, when I mentioned pepper, she immediately got up and went to the refrigerator to get the pepper. I turned my head and looked to the right. She knew I needed a tissue and immediately handed me one. After the meal, I glanced at the fruit table at the back and she immediately brought the fruit over. Whether it is with the children by our side or because they have grown up and live next to their respective schools, our husband-and-wife's "respect" can always be consistent. For example, before dinner, she placed all the dishes on the table and also placed two bowls, each with a spoon in the bowl. The curry rice feast started, I took one or two bites and said, "The round chicken legs are still sticky to the skin, so chopsticks should be more useful." She immediately got up and went to fetch them. I quickly stopped her and said:

"No, no, you eat yours."

"Have you decided not to use chopsticks?"

"I'm sorry to bother you to pick it up. If I want it, I'll go get it myself."

"I would love to," she said as she walked towards the cupboard and quickly brought me a pair of chopsticks.

From the above details, it is not difficult to infer how my wife strives to manage a happy and healthy family in her daily life.

Ever since our children were very young, she always used her holidays to take three children everywhere for sports, outings and studies. Three children walking on the road, often dressed in the same clothes, are extremely cute scenes, and I spend most of my time busy with my own affairs in the research room. Since the children entered elementary school, she usually took them to Japan on time to play and broaden their horizons, until one year, she just quietly followed and watched, letting the children plan and act on their own; After returning to Taiwan, she told me, "From now on, if our children want to go to Japan alone to play, I will also feel at ease." Therefore, most of the great credit for raising children should be attributed to my wife.

In terms of purchasing daily necessities, our husband-and-wife can be said to be a standard "couple in pairs". In fact, she had already obtained a car driver's license a long time ago, but she never drove and would rather let her skills deteriorate. She always arranges time, and I drive her to the big store. I am responsible for pushing the shopping cart, and she is responsible for purchasing. That's how it works for thirty years. Later on, if I occasionally drove alone to go shopping, it would seem strange, like a professional driver missing out on his passengers. Therefore, the interdependent lifestyle is very interesting, which does not need to be deliberately cultivated, but becomes natural over time.

I usually focus on my research at my desk, and when there are successful results, I usually go to mainland China or South Korea to publish papers. About one article is read out every year. But due to the fact that my wife had to be busy with household chores in her early years and the children were young, I was asked to go alone to Shijiazhuang, Chengde, Beijing, Xiamen, Beidaihe, Chongqing, Xi'an, Zhangzhou, and South Korea to publish papers. Later, the burden of household chores gradually eased, and I was finally able to take my wife with me; This is like having crops cultivated and waiting for both of us to harvest together happily. Therefore, regarding academic

activities, my wife and I have been to Yunnan, Guangxi, Hubei, Hunan, Gansu, Henan, Shanxi, Hebei, Shandong, Inner Mongolia, as well as Harbin, Shenyang, and also made a trip to North Korea. For a longer period of time, we lived at Beijing Normal University for academic research or served as visiting professors at Inner Mongolia University. She was my "accompanying family member"; This is the memory of our mutual assistance and hard work together.

Before checking out of our hotel, we will definitely tidy it up as if it has never been used before. This is the Japanese way my wife adopts; This greatly increased my dependence on her. As for the Mongolian grasslands, as a man who grew up in the countryside, I originally planned to buy horse riding tickets like most tourists, but my wife dared not ride, so I had to accompany her to buy a carriage ticket for us two. It was a middle-aged woman leading a thin and weak horse, pulling a carriage slowly forward. Compared to the vast cavalry, riding a slow carriage was really boring. However, on the one hand, I comfort myself from the heart, this is a time to hone my patience; On the other hand, I am happy for my wife because she was able to easily experience the grassland scenery by using the basic model. As long as she is happy, all the hardships along the way will disappear.

After a thorough review, I have come to a firm answer: "What a happy person I am! I must do my best to take care of and maintain this warm current situation." Director Li from the School of Engineering at our school once conveyed the reminder given to me by "experts", asking me not to violate taboos. I am sincerely grateful. But I don't need to trouble this "experts" to coach me, I am confident in my ability to solve problems. Therefore, I called the Libra girl and said, "My wife is retired and has moved down to live in the same dormitory with me. She is a Scorpio, you will understand." After saying these words, I have never been in contact with her since then, which should be considered easy for Libras to understand my heart and make me admire. In the end, we were both safe and sound.

In short, I think the "Constellation me" belongs to the "natural me" and the "cultivation me" belongs to the "civilization me". "Constellation me" accepts the pull of nature in some way. People of certain constellations have certain common thinking patterns with each other and understand and cherish each other. This is certainly a match made in heaven and is gratifying; but if people do not consider the actual situation around them, blindly relying on horoscope orientation may only cause people to stay in the "natural me" and lose the opportunity for self-excellence. Therefore, if you can cultivate yourself and evolve into a "civilization me", you will not only be able to maintain perfect harmony in the current situation around you, but you will also have the opportunity to sublimate your own soul. At this moment, I am obligated and happy to sublimate my soul.

Chapter 33   New Stage, New Journey

On February 11, 2023, when I returned to my hometown in Nantou, in order to tidy up the courtyard landscape, I sawed bamboo with a saw and worked continuously for several hours. Squatting and moving, squatting and sawing, the result are that my left knee is injured and suddenly feels like an electric shock, completely unable to withstand the force.

Soon, my left knee swelled up, and there seemed to be water inside. I went to a western pharmacy to buy some sore patch to apply on it, and also went to see a Chinese medicine doctor nearby. Acupuncture and moxibustion treatment for a week, but the effect was not obvious. A colleague told me that this injury may require more than a year of treatment and rest to recover. I suddenly felt frustrated. How could this be delayed for so long? I participate

in Teacher Ye Wenkuan's club two nights every week to practice Tai Chi Chuan and swordsmanship, and I always enjoy it. If I have to pause for a year, it is an unacceptable situation for me. Especially in the "double jump leg" movement of Tai Chi Knife, which involves jumping up and slapping the sneakers in front of me, my left knee must quickly recover.

The sudden pain of electric shock occurred four times in total, which was very terrifying. For example, when I was walking on a campus path, my left knee suddenly couldn't move, causing unbearable pain and unable to move a single step. I stand on one foot, lightly touching the ground with the tip of my left foot. Occasionally, students or outsiders walked slowly past me, and I felt panicked and embarrassed. I really didn't know what to do. I had to pick up my phone and focus on it, my fingers sliding and sliding, just pretending to be busy. My biggest concern is, if I happen to walk under the traffic light, even if the green light is on, do I dare to walk over? What should I do if I get stuck in the middle of the road, in that helpless and critical moment?

On Saturday, February 25th, the fourth electric shock pain occurred again. I stood by the roadside and called my wife, saying that as long as I could get into the car smoothly, I could drive to Linkou because my right foot could move freely. She contacted my second son to inform him about my knee condition and wanted him to take care of it.

My second son and his wife both graduated from Changgeng Medical College and both hold dual certificates of Chinese and Western medicine. They are currently doctors at Hualien Tzu Chi Hospital. On the evening of the 25th, they returned to live next to Changgeng in Linkou, which was a small vacation suite that we old couple had recently purchased for the youngs. On the morning of the 26th, I hobbled for ten minutes from my residence and took the elevator upstairs to find my son and daughter-in-law.

My son helped me find a convenient location and chair for treatment, and my daughter-in-law brought me boiling water to drink, using mugwort to heat my feet. Then help me feel my pulse, and each of them grabs one hand; After a while, the two exchanged positions and continued to check my pulse; Then exchange ideas. After the steps of pressing and rotating, acupuncture and moxibustion was performed from the top of the head to the insteps Two needles were inserted into the knee, and a total of 17 needles were inserted into the whole body. After the treatment was completed, they had to rush back to Hualien to continue their busy work, so they introduced me to go back to the south to see a famous doctor, who only treated me once and was cured.

In this way, I quickly returned to the Tai Chi Chuan club, where I practiced "pushing hands" more diligently. Its essence was: "Relaxed and flexible, combining hardness and softness; Adhere to and follow the other party; Don't lose, and don't confront." Not only did I stand by and watch others practicing swordsmanship, but my own 'double jump leg' also jumped up again.

In 2023, my son and daughter-in-law held a small wedding banquet in Taipei, inviting colleagues and classmates to participate. My wife and I happily entered the wedding banquet venue, marking a new journey in our lives.

On August 13, 2023, I published a paper at Shanxi University. I also delivered a speech at the opening ceremony as a Taiwanese scholar who cofounded the "Chinese Book of Songs Society" in Shijiazhuang, Hebei in 1993.

A Western poem that I will always remember in my heart:

My heart leaps up when I behold
A rainbow in the sky:
So was it, when my life began;
So is it now I am a man;
So be it when I shall grow old,
Or let me die!

--William Wordsworth's' Rainbow Poems'

Postscript

1. After writing this book, in terms of space ratio, I feel guilty that there are too few descriptions about my mother and my wife. In fact, they are the two most important people in my life. My mother lived to be 90. She loved me deeply with her life; and my wife loved me as deeply as she loved her own life. In addition, it is the love and care from the heart that my elder sisters and younger sister gave me. That kind of care was created by the outstanding upbringing of my parents. Family members who treat each other sincerely are enough to bring confidence and happiness in life. I have a very deep understanding of these beliefs.

2. I always hope that my book can bring readers a happy mood, but in reality, it may not be able to achieve this wish, and even make some readers feel a bit heavy or sad; I certainly don't like to see such results. Fortunately, according to recent research by chemists, when people cry due to emotions, these tears contain toxic chemicals. Tearing can help the body rid itself of toxic chemicals, thereby reducing the risk of heart disease. So, occasionally shedding tears is actually beneficial for health. If the opinions of these experts are credible, then the concerns I mentioned above seem unnecessary.

3. Under the current trend of internationalization, university teachers must cooperate with the "all English" policy. Given that some academic data on ancient phonetics is listed at the end of the first unit of this book, I am concerned that the general translator may not be able to accurately express my original meaning in the simplest words and sentences due to unfamiliarity with professional knowledge; Therefore, I have decided to handle the relevant issues myself. In late July this year, I devoted myself to writing the entire book in English during the summer vacation. If I

occasionally do not adopt literal translation, it may be due to cultural differences between China and the West (such as puns not being effective), which forces me to exercise the discretion of the "original author" and make slight changes to the sentence. The Chinese version of the book is titled "鹿鳴呦呦", while the English version is titled "*Deer Bleating Sound Yo Yo*". In line with the original intention of keeping up with the trend of the times, I did not reflect on my own clumsiness, but wrote in English. I hope that I can throw bricks and attract jade. I also hope that wise people will give me their valuable advices. In addition, I would like to express my special gratitude to Baidu and Google, who are my consulting partners.

- End of the entire book –

國家圖書館出版品預行編目資料

Deer Bleating Sound Yo Yo／Lin Yeh Lien　著 —初版—
臺中市：天空數位圖書　2024.01
面：17*23 公分
ISBN：978-626-7161-87-6（平裝）

書　　　名：Deer Bleating Sound Yo Yo
發 行 人：蔡輝振
出 版 者：天空數位圖書有限公司
作　　　者：Lin Yeh Lien
美工設計：設計組
版面編輯：採編組
出版日期：2024 年 1 月（初版）
銀行名稱：合作金庫銀行南台中分行
銀行帳戶：天空數位圖書有限公司
銀行帳號：006–1070717811498
郵政帳戶：天空數位圖書有限公司
劃撥帳號：22670142
定　　　價：新台幣 580 元整
電子書發明專利第　Ｉ　306564　號

服務項目：個人著作、學位論文、學報期刊等出版印刷及DVD製作
影片拍攝、網站建置與代管、系統資料庫設計、個人企業形象包裝與行銷
影音教學與技能檢定系統建置、多媒體設計、電子書製作及客製化等
TEL　：(04)22623893　　　　MOB：0900602919
FAX　：(04)22623863
E-mail：familysky@familysky.com.tw
Https ://www.familysky.com.tw/
地　　址：台中市南區忠明南路 787 號 30 樓國王大樓
No.787-30, Zhongming S. Rd., South District, Taichung City 402, Taiwan (R.O.C.)